Deutscher Designer Club

INHALT

VORWORT 4
ES LEBEN DIE LETZTEN 10% 6
IN EIGENER SACHE 8

GRAND PRIX 10

DAS GUTE NETZWERK
GOLD 24
SILBER 30
BRONZE 36
AWARD 44

EHRENMITGLIED SIGI MAYER 50
NACHRUF ALBRECHT GRAF GOERTZ 68

DAS GUTE STÜCK
GOLD 76
SILBER 92
BRONZE 126
AWARD 202

JURY 294

ZUKUNFT 308

INDEX 318
AUFLISTUNG DESIGNAGENTUREN 341
DDC IMPRESSUM 348

CONTENTS

FOREWORD 4
LONG LIVE THE FINAL 10% 6
ON OUR OWN ACCOUNT 8

GRAND PRIX 10

THE GOOD NETWORK
GOLD 24
SILBER 30
BRONZE 36
AWARD 44

HONORARY MEMBER SIGI MAYER 50
OBITUARY ALBRECHT GRAF GOERTZ 68

THE GOOD PIECE
GOLD 76
SILBER 92
BRONZE 126
AWARD 202

JURY 294

ZUKUNFT 308

INDEX 318
DESIGN AGENCIES 341
DDC IMPRINT 348

Der Deutsche Designer Club (DDC) ist eine Initiative, die die Botschaft ausgezeichneter Gestaltung in Deutschland und über die Grenzen hinweg verbreiten möchte.

Speziell ist der Club eine Plattform für interdisziplinäre Gestalter. Besonders soll die Qualität der vernetzten, integrierten Kommunikation über alle Gestaltungs-Disziplinen und Medien hinweg gepflegt und gefördert werden. Die gegenseitige Akzeptanz, die Schnittstellen, der Abbau der „Sprachlosigkeit", die Kommunikation der Gestalter untereinander, mit Ausbildungsstätten und nicht zuletzt mit unseren Auftraggebern soll mit Hilfe unterschiedlicher Kommunikations-Plattformen und Aktionen verbessert werden.

Damit ergibt sich die klare Positionierung: Der Deutsche Designer Club (DDC) ist der Club der interdisziplinären Gestalter.

The German Designer Club (DDC) is an initiative that wants to spread the message of design excellence in Germany and beyond. Above all, the Club is a platform for interdisciplinary designers.

In particular, we want to cultivate and promote the quality of networked, integrated communication throughout all design disciplines and media. Mutual acceptance, interfaces, the reduction of "speechlessness", communication among designers, with trading facilities, and of course with clients are to be improved with the aid of various communication platforms and campaigns.

The resulting positioning is clear: The German Designer Club (DDC) is a Club of interdisciplinary designers.

Thomas Feicht
Präsident Deutscher Designer Club (DDC),
President of the German Designer Club (DDC)

VORWORT

ES LEBEN DIE LETZTEN 10 %.

Das Wörtchen 100 % (gar 110 %) ist schnell in den Mund genommen. ALLE wollen das. Perfektion halt. Wenn wir nach Beispielen suchen – apple fällt uns ein – mit einer Klitzekleinigkeit – dem orange-grün leuchtenden Ring am Netzstecker. Müsste nicht sein. Ist aber gut. In Deutschland, im Mittelstand liegen die Klassiker ganz schnell auf der Zunge: ERCO, FSB und vitra. Aber da sollte es doch mehr Marken, Firmen geben. Damit wir das Lob gleichmäßiger verteilen, auch andere Mittelständler loben, die es verdient haben. Gutes, Vernetztes, Ganzheitliches also.

Fangen wir doch ausnahmsweise bei C an, bei Carl Mertens. Vielleicht eine zu große, aber sehr konsequente Produktpalette (auch der DDC schneidet sein Brot damit – Sie merken wir sind bei Bestecken). Also gutes Produkt-Design. Und damit fing auch alles an. Es folgte ein unaufgeregtes Corporate Design, klare Packungen und jetzt emotionale Fotografie aus der Produktion obendrauf. Für Katalog und Kommunikation. Dazu das Internet. Ein schlichtes Portal (www.carl-mertens.com). Also ich hätte es gerne gemacht. Gratulation und jetzt noch 10 % Erfolg obendrauf.

LONG LIVE THE FINAL 10 %.

100 % (or even 110 %) is easily said. After all EVERYONE wants perfection. If we look for examples involving ingenious details: Apple springs to mind – with the luminous orange-green ring on the mains plug. Not earth-shattering. But good. In Germany, in the mid-tier sector, the classics are quickly named: ERCO, FSB and vitra. But there are surely more brands, more firms deserving of mention. To ensure that we allocate praise more evenly, also lauding other mid-tier companies who've earned it. With harmoniously holistic excellence.

For a change, let's start with C, with Carl Mertens. A product range that might perhaps be too large, but one of aesthetic rigor (DDC cuts with it as well – as you will notice, we're dealing with cutlery here). So we're talking good product design, and that's where it all began. Followed by unfussy corporate design, clear packaging and now some emotional photography from the production process. For catalogue and communication. Plus the internet. An elegantly simple portal (www.carl-mertens.com). One I would be proud to have created. Congratulations and now 10 % extra success into the bargain.

Museum für Angewandte Kunst Frankfurt

IN EIGENER SACHE...

Wann ist eine Corporate Identity gelungen etabliert? Wenn sie niemand mehr wahrnimmt? Wenn sie sofort erkennbar ist? Seit der Einführung unserer neuen CI im März 2005 verging kaum ein Tag, an dem nicht mit Lob und Tadel, heiß und kalt darüber geurteilt wurde. Ausgewiesene Experten und ausgesprochene Laien äußerten sich gleichermaßen vehement positiv oder negativ über das Vorgehen des von uns beauftragten Teams vier5 (Paris und auf Reisen).

Was ist geschehen? Vier5 führte unsere spezielle Museumsschrift, 025aPlotter, ein, kreierte ein ausführliches Manual über zukünftige Drucksachen- und Informationsgestaltung und schuf als Logo eine Schriftmarke. Und in geradezu paritätischer Polarisierung wird seither die Schrift als sehr gut lesbar oder als Zumutung bezeichnet und die Kataloge, Poster und Einladungen als klassisch schön oder potthässlich benannt. Das Logo, die Schriftmarke steht im Zentrum des Interesses. Viel Lob und beleidigende Invektiven bis hin zur Bemerkung von der entarteten Schrift, aber auch wieder in ausgeglichenen Quantitäten. Das überraschende Merkmal unserer neuen CI ist, dass seit fast zwei Jahren die Diskussion nicht abreißt. Wir wollen mit der Wortmarke, die durch scheinbares Überdrucken den immer neu zu überdenkenden Begriff der Angewandten Kunst in den Mittelpunkt rückt, zeigen, dass man hier nie zu einer gültigen Begriffsklärung kommt. Deswegen sehen wir die neue CI als Teil einer kontinuierlichen Diskussion um die Aufgaben unseres Hauses zwischen Kunst und Handwerk und Design. Auch Schriftkunst und Kommunikationsdesign sind Angewandte Künste und müssen zur heftigen Diskussion anregen. Solche Dispute wünsche ich auch den Damen und Herren, die im diesjährigen DDC Jahrbuch 07 Erwähnung finden. Diskussion ist allemal besser als gefällige Harmonie.

Professor Dr. Ulrich Schneider
Direktor des Museums für Angewandte Kunst Frankfurt

ON OUR OWN ACCOUNT ...

When has a corporate identity been successfully established? When people no longer notice it? When it's immediately recognisable? Since the introduction of our new CI in March of 2005, hardly a single day has gone by on which verdicts have not been passed, expressing praise and censure, liking and loathing. Knowledgeable experts and absolute laypersons have voiced both vehement approval and equally vehement disapproval of the contribution from vier5, the team we commissioned (Paris and itinerant).

What has happened? Vier5 introduced our special museum font, 025aPlotter, created a comprehensive manual on future printed-matter and information design, and came up with a distinctive logo. And in a veritable parity of polarisation, the font has since then been described as highly legible or as an affront, and the catalogues, posters and invitations as classically elegant or ugly as sin. The logo is the focus of interest. Much praise, much vituperative invective, even a remark on a "degenerate" font, but once again in balanced quantities.

The surprising feature of our new CI is that for almost two years now the discussion has not subsided. With the logo, which by apparent overprinting puts the focus on the need to continually rethink the concept of applied art, we aim to show that here a definitive semantic clarification is never achieved. This is why we see the new CI as part of a continuous debate centred around our organisation's remit between art and craftsmanship and design.

Calligraphy and communication design are also applied arts, and inevitably give rise to heated debate. And my wish is for disputes of this nature to come the way of the ladies and gentlemen mentioned in this year's DDC Annual for 2007. Discussion is always better than complacent harmony.

Professor Dr. Ulrich Schneider
Director of the Museum for Applied Art
Frankfurt

GRAND PRIX

AUDI.
VORSPRUNG ENTSTEHT
ZUERST IM KOPF.

Der Deutsche Designer Club zeichnet die
Audi AG für ihre außerordentliche Arbeit in
den Bereichen Design, Kommunikation,
Messeauftritt, Internetgestaltung und Marken-
führung aus. Nur wenigen Unternehmen ist
es in den letzten Jahren gelungen, eine Marke
und ihre Werte so konsequent zu vermitteln
und sie sowohl inhaltlich als auch emotional
in die Tat umzusetzen. Audi beweist seine
Haltung Tag für Tag. Audi lebt seine Premiumstrategie – vom Schreibtisch des Vorstandes bis
in den Showroom.

AUDI.
EXCELLENCE STARTS
IN THE CREATIVE MIND.

The German Designer Club honours Audi AG
for its exceptional work in the fields of design,
communication, trade fair interfacing, website
creation and brand management. Not many
companies in recent years have succeeded in
communicating a brand and its values so pur-
posefully, with such substantive and emotional
impact. Day in, day out, Audi validates its
mindset. Audi lives out its premium strategy –
from the director's desktop to the showroom.

Markenbuch für Führungskräfte der Audi AG als inhaltlicher und emotionaler Leitfaden für (Selbst-) Verständnis und Wertevermittlung der Marke Audi / Brand book for Audi AG's senior managers and other executives as a guideline, both content-related and emotional, on how to understand the Audi brand (and themselves) and communicate its values to the outside world. Designagentur / Designagency **Mutabor Design GmbH**

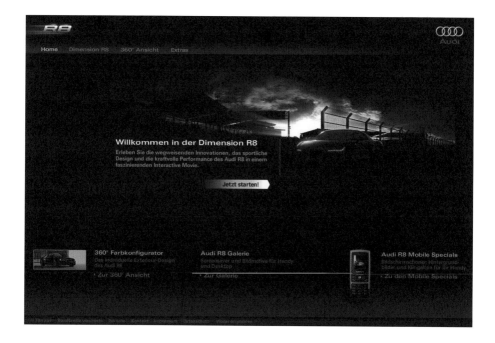

Microsite zum Launch des Sportwagens von Audi R8. / Microsite to introduce the sports car R8 by AUDI (http://www.audi.de/R8). Designagentur / Designagency **argonauten G2 GmbH**

Website als Teil der Launchkampagne für die zweite Generation des Audi TT. / Website as part of the campaign to introduce the second generation of the AUDI TT (http://www.audi.de/TT). Designagentur / Designagency **argonauten G2 GmbH**

GRAND PRIX

 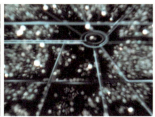 

Mediale Inszenierung des TT auf dem design annual 2006. / Media-based presentation of the TT at the 2006 design annual. Designagentur / Designagency **Mutabor Design GmbH**

GRAND PRIX

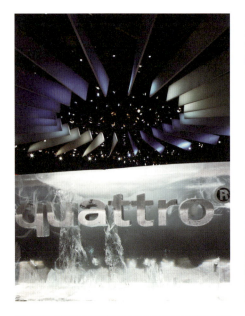

Messeauftritt der Marke Audi für A-Messen. / Presentation for of the Audi brand all of the top international trade fairs. Designagentur / Designagency **Mutabor Design GmbH**

DAS GUTE NETZWERK

DAS GUTE NETZWERK

GOLD

MotoCross Journalism Adventure

Aufgabe / Briefing: Motorola ist Pionier, Innovator und Visionär von Kommunikationstechnik und versteht sich als Vorreiter der Seamless Mobility. Ziel ist es diese Identität 40 internationalen Journalisten aus den Bereichen Lifestyle und Technologie zu vermitteln. **Umsetzung:** Das Motocross Journalism Adventure greift die Vision der nahtlosen Kommunikation auf und übersetzt sie analog in die Natur der Schweizer Berge. Auf spielerische Art und durch das Verschmelzen medialer Produkte wird Seamless Mobility erlebbar.

Thema / Subject **Event** • Auftraggeber / Client **Leipziger & Partner PR GmbH** • Designagentur / Designagency **Another Romeo TM Design**

Assignment / Briefing: Motorola is pioneer, innovator and visionary in communication technology and understands itself as precursor of seamless mobility. The aim was to communicate this identity to 40 international journalists in the fields of lifestyle and technology. **Implementation:** The Motocross Journalism Adventure adapts the vision of seamless mobility, analogically translating it into the nature of the Swiss Mountains. In a playful way and through the blending of multimedia products, seamless mobility can be experienced.

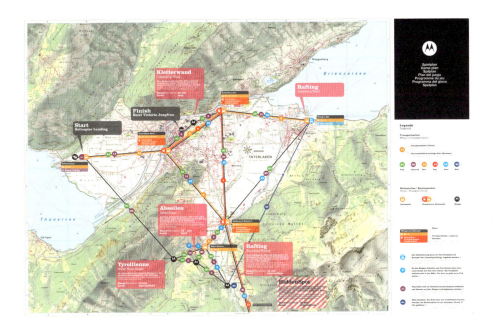

# SILBER

Adidas GMM Locker Room

Aufgabe / Briefing: Präsentation der wichtigsten Kernthemen aus allen Sportsegmenten von adidas für Händler, Wiederverkäufer, Mitarbeiter und Fachbranche in einem Instant Showroom auf dem adidas GMM (General Marketing Meeting), Dauer: 3 Tage. **Umsetzung:** GET DRESSED FOR 2006; Die Umkleidekabine als Showroom. Die Prototypen der Produkte – drapiert, als ob die Athleten „eben zum Duschen" rausgegangen sind. Hinter den Spindtüren: Die Erlebnisbereiche – jeder Raum eine begehbare Kampagne aus Grafik, Film und Produktpräsentation.

Thema / Subject **Sportartikel / Instant Showroom** • Auftraggeber / Client **Adidas GMM Locker Room** • Designagentur / Designagency **Mutabor Design GmbH**

Assignment / Briefing: To present the most important key topics from all of adidas's sport segments for dealers, retailers, employees and the specialist trade in an Instant Showroom at the adidas GMM (General Marketing Meeting); duration 3 days. **Implementation:** GET DRESSED FOR 2006; the locker room as the showroom. The product prototypes – draped, as though the athletes had just gone out "to take a shower". Behind the locker doors we find the theme areas – each room is a walk-in campaign consisting of graphics, a film and a product presentation.

NICHTS IST SPANNENDER
UNBERECHENBARER ALS EINE

HERAUSFORDERNDER UND
FILM ZU MACHEN.

Rainer Gehrisch, Gehrisch+Krack Filmproduktions AG

www.gk-film.de

Voraus denken. Mercedes-Benz auf der IAA Frankfurt 2005.

Aufgabe / Briefing: 7.000 Quadratmeter Ausstellung, 900.000 Besucher, durchschnittlich 45 Minuten Besuchsdauer und eine Weltpremiere: Der Auftritt von Mercedes-Benz auf der IAA 2005 verlangt eine klare Dramaturgie. **Umsetzung:** Auf 15 Minuten Erleben der Produktpalette folgen 30 Exklusivminuten für die neue S-Klasse: In der inszenierten Begegnung mit dem luxuriösen Marken-Flaggschiff werden konzentriert die Markenwerte von Mercedes-Benz kommuniziert.

Thema / Subject **Messeauftritt** • Auftraggeber / Client **DaimlerChrysler AG**
Architektur / Architecture **Kauffmann Theilig & Partner Freie Architekten BDA**
Kommunikation / Communication **Atelier Markgraph GmbH**

Assignment / Briefing: 7,000 square meters of floor space, 900,000 visitors, each of whom spent an average 45 minutes on the booth, a long-awaited world premiere – the Mercedes-Benz presentation at the IAA 2005 demanded a clear dramatic structure. **Implementation:** Fifteen minutes to look around, thirty for the S-Klasse – in a meticulously-planned rendezvous with the brand flagship, visitors experience the innovative power, passion and quality of Mercedes-Benz in their most concentrated form.

DAS GUTE NETZWERK

BRONZE

Wetterpark Offenbach

Aufgabe / Briefing: Konzeption und Entwicklung einer permanenten Ausstellung im öffentlichen Raum auf einer brachliegenden Fläche von 20.000 qm für die Stadt Offenbach, den Planungsverband Rhein-Main und den DWD. Das Projekt umfasst die redaktionelle Erarbeitung der Inhalte, die Konzeption und den Entwurf der Exponate sowie die Integration und Planung des Landschaftsraums – in der Verbindung aus Informations- und Produktdesign, Architektur und Landschaftsplanung.

Thema / Subject **Wetterpark** • Auftraggeber / Client **Planungsverband Ballungsraum Rhein-Main, Stadt Offenbach, DWD** • Designagentur / Designagency **unit-design**

Assignment / Briefing: The conception for the redevelopment of a wasteland area of 20,000 sqm into a permanent open-air exhibition, open to the public, for the town Offenbach, the Planungsverband Rhein-Main and the DWD. The project encompassed the editorial drafting of the contents, the concept, and the blueprints for the exhibits, as well as the integration and planning of the landscape areas – in the combination of information and product design, architecture and landscape planning.

Umsetzung: Durch Exponatinstallationen und erläuternde Grafiken werden dem Besucher die komplexen Zusammenhänge des Wetters und deren wissenschaftliche Hintergründe in verständlicher Weise vermittelt. Die sinnliche Wahrnehmung der vielfältigen Erscheinungsformen des Wetters und ihre Wirkung auf den Menschen wird durch die Aufforderung zu aktiver Beobachtung oder Interaktion gefördert. Die Gestaltung der Elemente sollte die bestehende Umgebung möglichst unangetastet lassen. Als verbindendes gestalterisches Element für die Exponatstationen dienen Holzstege, die vom Weg in die Landschaft hinausstechen und zu den Exponaten mit Grafik- und Texterläuterung führen.

Implementation: The exhibit installations and explanatory graphics convey the visitors the complex coherences of the weather and their scientific background in an understandable way. The sensual perception of the weather's various appearances and their effect on people is encouraged by active observation and interaction. The elements' aesthetic should leave their environment as untouched as possible. A wooden path is used as connecting aesthetic element for the exhibit stations, which stands out from the landscape and leads to the exhibits with explanatory graphics and text.

BRONZE

„Walk of Ideas" – ein Spaziergang durch Ideen aus Deutschland

Aufgabe / Briefing: Die WM 2006 lenkt die Blicke der ganzen Welt auf Deutschland. Spektakuläre Bilder, an denen kein Tourist und kein Kamerateam vorbeikommen, sollen Deutschland als ein „Land der Ideen" der Weltöffentlichkeit präsentieren. **Umsetzung:** Vor den Wahrzeichen Berlins werden sechs Großskulpturen aufgestellt, die Ideentradition und die anhaltende Innovationskraft in Deutschland inszenieren. Gemeinsam bilden sie den „Walk of Ideas" – die größte öffentliche Ausstellung ihrer Art.

Thema / Subject **Kommunikation von Deutschland als „Land der Ideen"** • Auftraggeber / Client **FC Deutschland GmbH** • Designagentur / Designagency **Scholz & Friends Sensai**

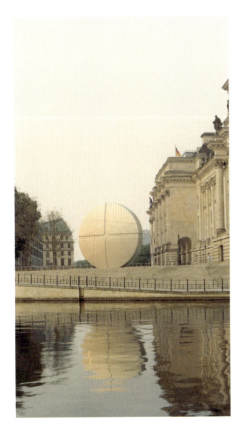

Assignment / Briefing: During the World Cup 2006 the nations of the world are looking at Germany. The country is presenting itself as a "Land of Ideas" with spectacular pictures, that no tourists or camera team can leave aside. **Implementation:** Six oversized sculptures will be placed in front of Berlin landmarks, representing Germany's tradition of ideas and the continuous power of innovation. Together, they form the "Walk of Ideas" – one of the largest public exhibitions of its kind.

AWARD

Oerlikon – We are one

Aufgabe / Briefing: Ein global agierendes Unternehmen mit Schweizer Herkunft setzt neue Zeichen. OC Oerlikon repräsentiert die Neuausrichtung als globaler Premium-Hightech-Konzern und greift zugleich die Schweizer Tradition des Unternehmens auf. **Umsetzung:** Auf Basis der Neuausrichtung wurde die Markenarchitektur und das Corporate Design entwickelt. Unter der kommunikativen Leitidee WE ARE ONE werden Vision und Werte etabliert.

Thema / Subject **Corporate Design** • Auftraggeber / Client **OC Oerlikon Management AG**
Designagentur / Designagency **Claus Koch™**

Assignment / Briefing: A globally active company with Swiss origins is making its mark. OC Oerlikon stands for its reorientation as a global premium high-tech company and at the same time points to the Swiss tradition of the company. **Implementation:** The brand architecture and the corporate design were developed on the basis of the reorientation. Vision and values are established under the communicative key idea WE ARE ONE.

Die Audi Messekommunikation: „Audi A-Messe-Konzept"

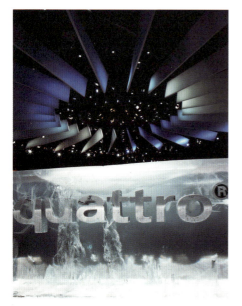

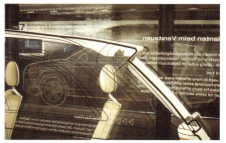

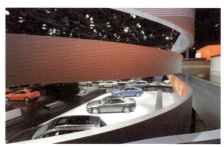

Aufgabe / Briefing: Jeder Messeauftritt bietet die Chance, die Marke Audi und die Produkte an einem Ort zu erleben. Die gesamte Inszenierung soll die Marke Audi darstellen und das Highlight-Produkt emotional präsentieren. **Umsetzung:** Eine individuelle Kommunikationsarchitektur für jede der internationalen A-Messen, die den kommunikativen und inszenatorischen Fokus auf das jeweilige Highlight legt.

Thema / Subject **Automobil** • Auftraggeber / Client **Audi AG** • Designagentur / Designagency **Mutabor Design GmbH**

Assignment / Briefing: Every trade fair provides the opportunity to experience the Audi brand and products in one place. The entire presentation is designed to stage the Audi brand and present the highlight product in an emotional way. **Implementation:** An individual communication architecture for all of the top international trade fairs that puts the communicative and presentational focus on the trade fairs' respective highlight.

DAS EHRENMITGLIED

Sigi Mayer

„Ich mach' viel in Werbung, Architektur und Film. Man kann von mir auch ein Büro ausgestattet haben, nicht bloß eine Printkampagne, oder mich auch als Kreativberater tageweise engagieren."

"I do a lot of work in advertising, architecture and films. You can also have me furnish your office, not just handle a print campaign, or hire me by the day as a creative consultant."

bei Brigitta Zettl /

In Ewigkeit, Damen.

Los.

Zettl GmbH
A-4064 Oftering, Lehnerstraße 1

Telefon
+ 43 7221/63981-0
Telefax
+ 43 7221/639816

Internet:
www.zettlgmbh.at
e-mail:
office@zettlgmbh.at

DAS NEUE DDC EHRENMITGLIED: SIGI MAYER

DER QUERDENKER.

Sigi Mayer der Linzer Querdenker studierte an der Wiener Akademie der Künste. Er beschloss jedoch schon bald der bildenden Kunst den Rücken zu kehren und sich als Werber zu betätigen. Heute entsteht in seiner Kreativschmiede erfolgreiche und sehr ungewöhnliche Werbung. Oft wird er auch als Werbe-Outlaw bezeichnet. International anerkannt verkneift er es sich nicht für lokale Kunden wie den Fleischer Anton Riepl, den Geschenkeversand Zettl GmbH oder für die Grazer Drogenberatungsstelle ungewöhnliche Ideen durch alle Disziplinen zu entwickeln und zu realisieren, die weltweit in Wettbewerben hoch dekoriert werden.

Sigi Mayer ist als Werber Autodidakt. Sein Geld hat er zu Anfang als bildender Künstler, dann als Grafiker, Verpackungsgestalter und Möbeldesigner verdient. Er sagt selbst über sich: „Ich bin ein rotes Tuch für die Branche, weil ich die Regeln der Werbung brechen will."

So manchen Kollegen wirft er Angst vor dem Kunden vor - der Kreative sollte immer der Regisseur sein, nicht der Kunde. London ist für ihn seit vielen Jahren ein wichtiger Ort zum Sammeln von Eindrücken. Mit den Kollegen in England fühlt er sich sehr verbunden, sie sind mutig und kreativ. **Norbert Herold von Heye & Partner München verdanken wir durch seine Laudatio (folgend) anlässlich der Verleihung der Ehrenmitgliedschaft des Deutschen Designer Clubs (DDC) an Sigi Mayer eine sehr treffende Beschreibung.**

THE LATERAL THINKER.

Sigi Mayer, the lateral thinker from Linz, studied at the Viennese Academy of Fine Arts. Very soon, though, he decided to turn his back on the plastic arts and devote himself to advertising. Today, he's the brooding creator of successful and highly unusual advertising. He's often described as one of the sector's outlaws. Though he enjoys an international reputation, he's quite happy to develop and implement out-of-the-ordinary, cross-disciplinary ideas (prize-winning concepts in competitions the whole world over) for local clients like the butcher Anton Riepl, the gift mail order firm Zettl GmbH or for the Drugs Advice Bureau in Graz. As an advertising professional, Sigi Mayer is self-taught. He started off earning his money in the plastic arts, then as a graphics creator, and as a packaging and furniture designer. His own verdict on himself is: "I enrage the whole sector, because I aim to break the rules of advertising." Some of his colleagues, he accuses, are frightened of their clients – but the creative talent should always be in charge, not the client. For many years now, he has revered London as an important place for conceptual stimulation: he feels close ties with his counterparts in England, they are bold and creative. **Norbert Herold of Heye & Partner in Munich has provided a highly apposite description in his laudatio (next page) on the occasion of Sigi Mayer's being awarded honorary membership of the German Designer Club (DDC).**

Meine sehr verehrten Damen und Herren, liebe Kollegen vom DDC.

Ich möchte Sie warnen – vor einem Mann aus Linz. Er ist Art Director, Regisseur, Architekt, Möbeldesigner, Packungsgestalter, Typograph und Unruheherd. Er ist anstrengend, ungemütlich und nervös. Er sucht keine Kunden, Kunden suchen ihn. Entweder sie unterwerfen sich ihm - oder sie gehen wieder. Aber wer sich auf ihn einlässt, bekommt am Ende etwas, was niemand sonst hat, etwas Unerhörtes, Ungesehenes, Einzigartiges, Provokatives, Schönes – etwas mit Charakter. Er hat als einziger Gestalter aus dem deutschsprachigen Raum beim strengsten Gestaltungswettbewerb, dem britischen D&AD Award mehrfach den begehrten Pencil erhalten, bei einer Einsendemenge von 24.000-26.000 Arbeiten. Weil er alles, alles anders macht als andere, um dann kopiert zu werden. So wurde er der meist kopierte Art Director und Typograph Österreichs.

So einer wie er ist entweder in New York oder London an der Spitze - oder Grantler in Linz. Es gehört wohl zu den österreichischen Eigenarten, in Linz zu leiden vorzuziehen. So sind die Kunden denn auch ein bisschen kleiner als in den Metropolen, es gehört auch eine Bäckerei dazu. Angenommen, Sie wären dieser Bäcker, dann hätten Sie jetzt schwarze Brötchentüten. Ach, und ihre Bäckerei wäre außen auch schwarz – Ich kann Sie also nur warnen vor Sigi Mayer.

Nein, die Wahrheit ist natürlich: Die Wahl von Sigi Mayer ist für den DDC als Club mit Charakter eine große Ehre. Lieber Sigi, ich finde, es trifft den Richtigen, und ich hoffe, Du sagst – „dös taugt mer."

Ministerium
für
Unternehmenskultur

Landstraße 84/3
4020 Linz
www.mfuk.at

Ladies and gentlemen, esteemed colleagues of the DDC.

I should like to warn you – against a man from Linz. He is an art director, a producer, an architect, a furniture and packaging designer, a typographer and a troublemaker. He is finical, prickly and highly-strung. He doesn't look for clients – they seek him out. Either they give him free rein – or they go elsewhere. But those who put themselves in his hands ultimately get something that no one else has, something hitherto undreamed of, unseen, unique, provocative, beautiful – something with character. He is the only designer from the German-speaking countries to have repeatedly won the coveted pencil at the most exacting design competition of them all, the British D&AD Award, from among 24,000 – 26,000 entries. Because he does absolutely everything differently from all the others – who then start to imitate him. That's how he's become the most-copied art director and typographer in Austria.

Someone like him is either at the top of the tree in New York or London - or a curmudgeon in Linz. It must be a peculiarly Austrian idiosyncrasy to prefer suffering in Linz. For instance, the customers there are a bit smaller than in the big cities, in fact one of them's a bakery. Supposing you were this baker, you would now have black paper bags to sell your rolls in. Oh, and the outside of your bakery would be black as well – I can only warn you against Sigi Mayer. No, the truth is, of course: the choice of Sigi Mayer is a great honour for the DDC, as a club for genuine characters. My dear Sigi, I know this accolade is thoroughly deserved, and I hope you say – "I fit in here".

beerenberg(Bio)

Helmut
Brunner
Pachmayrstraße 127
4040 Linz
T. 0732-733095
www.beerenberg.at

Heidelbeere
(Vaccinium corymbosum)

Blaubeere
Kulturheidelbeere
Gartenheidelbeere
Blueberry

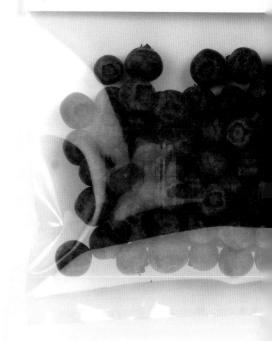

Helmut
Brunner
Pachmayrstraße 127
4040 Linz
T. 0732-733095
www.beerenberg.at

Heidelbeere
(Vaccinium corymbosum)

Blaubeere
Kulturheidelbeere
Gartenheidelbeere
Blueberry

Männer schlachten,
Frauen kochen – oder/

///// Produktion ist Männerdomäne,
      Gastronomie und Geschäfte
      sind Frauendomäne
///// 7 Lehrlinge
Die verschiedenen Geschäftsbereiche
weisen eine unterschiedliche
Geschlechterverteilung auf. Während
bei Produktion und Schlachtung fast
ausschließlich Männer beschäftigt
sind, sind in Büro, Gastronomie und
Detailgeschäften in erster Linie
Frauen angestellt. Derzeit sind im
Betrieb 7 Lehrlinge beschäftigt,
vier davon in der Produktion, zwei
in den Geschäften und ein Lehrling
im Büro. Auch bei der Beschäftigung
junger Menschen ist die Fleischmanufaktur Riepl ein verantwortungs-
voller Arbeitgeber. Sollte es einmal
vorkommen, dass jemand die Lehre
nicht schafft, ist der Arbeitgeber
bemüht, dass der oder die Betroffene
als Hilfsarbeitskraft im Betrieb
verbleiben kann.

Nachhaltigkeitsbericht /
der
Fleischmanufaktur
Anton Riepl

100% 100% Report

haltigkeitsbericht /

hrnanufaktur
Riepl

page 67

bei Brigitta Zetil / Seite – 26

Die neuen Wilden

– – Leckstein

Holzkassette 27x20x8 cm
Hussitenkugeln 3 Stück
– – *Lebzelterei Lubinger*

Karton mit Espressokaffee 250 g

Justino's Madeira Wine 0,375 l
– – *Vinhos Justino Henriques*

€ 29,00 / Best.Nr. 06027

– – Höhenkoller

Holzkassette 27x20x8 cm
Edelweiss-Nudeln 200 g

Kürbiskern-Pesto 106 ml

handgemachtes Edelweiß-Konfekt 5 Stück

€ 23,50 / Best.Nr. 06028

Die neuen Wilden

– – granitgeprüft

Holzkassette 36x18x10 cm
Junge Löwen 0,75 l
– – *Weinbäuerin Heidi Schröck*

Mühlviertler Granitspeck ca. 500 g

Mozzarino 190 ml – Weichkäse

handgeschöpfte Schokolade 65 g
– – *Schokoladenmanufaktur Zotter*

€ 39,00 / Best.Nr. 06029

ALBRECHT GRAF GOERTZ †

Tassilo von Grolman

Ehrenvorsitzender
und Gründer des
Deutschen Designer Clubs
(DDC) zum Tod von
Albrecht Graf Goertz.

Honorary Chairman
and Founder of the
German Designer Club
(DDC).

EIN MEISTER DES STILS

Albrecht Graf Goertz, Ehrenmitglied des DDC, verstarb am 27. Oktober 2006 im Alter von 92 Jahren. Autokenner denken bei diesem Namen sofort an den legendären BMW 507, jenen unvergleichlich elegant gezeichneten Sportwagen von 1955, der bis heute als das Meisterwerk im Automobil Design gilt und den Durchbruch für den Designer bedeutete.

1914 als Sohn eines alten Adelsgeschlechts im niedersächsischen Brunkensen geboren, absolvierte Goertz eine Banklehre bei der Deutschen Bank in Frankfurt, die er später in London bei einer Privatbank fortsetzte. Doch seine wahre Leidenschaft galt dem Automobil. 1935 emigriert er in die USA und begeistert sich in New York für das spektakuläre Auftunen alter Ford-Modelle. Bereits 1939 wird das Paragon-Coupé, sein erstes eigenes Design, auf der Weltausstellung in San Francisco präsentiert, das ihm Jahre später eine folgenreiche Bekanntschaft zum Stardesigner Raymond Loewy verschafft. Der erkennt sein Talent und verhilft ihm zu einem Designstudium am bekannten Pratt Institute in Brooklyn. Goertz arbeitet als Junior Designer in Loewys Studebaker-Entwicklungsabteilung und bei Norman Bel Geddes, bis er sich 1953 mit Goertz Industrial Design Inc. in New York selbständig macht. Einer der ersten großen Kunden ist Hohner, für die er Akkordeons und Mundharmonikas für den US-Markt gestaltet. Aber Autos bleiben die große Liebe von Goertz.

A MASTER OF STYLE

Albrecht Count Goertz, an honorary member of the DDC, passed away on 27 October 2006 at the age of 92. Car buffs, when they hear his name, think immediately of the legendary BMW 507, that incomparably elegant sports car of 1955, which even today is recognised as a masterpiece of automotive design and constituted a major breakthrough for Count Goertz.

Born in Brunkensen, Lower Saxony, in 1914 as the son of an old noble family, Goertz served an apprenticeship at Deutsche Bank in Frankfurt, which he later continued at a private bank in London. But his true passion was for cars. In 1935, he emigrated to the USA, and in New York developed an enthusiasm for spectacular tuning of old Ford models. By 1939, he had

Er lernt Max Hoffmann kennen, den wichtigsten amerikanischen Importeur für Luxusfahrzeuge aus Übersee, der ihm den Kontakt zu BMW vermittelt. Er gestaltet den BMW 503 Sportwagen, der große Zustimmung findet. Der BMW 507 aber ist 1955 auf der Automobilausstellung in Frankfurt der große Star – und Goertz der neue Star am Designerhimmel. Sein Name wird nun mit Größen wie Pinin Farina, Bertone, aber auch Raymond Loewy genannt.

Nicht nur für die Automobilbranche setzt Goertz Maßstäbe. Er gestaltet ebenso Büro- und Elektrogeräte, Fotoapparate, Radios und Fernsehgeräte, aber auch Möbel, Schmuck und Mode. Er ist ein interdisziplinärer Designer. 1989 kehrt er im Alter von 75 Jahren in seine alte Heimat zurück. Er wird Berater verschiedener Firmen und lehrt als Referent an Universitäten. In Brunkensen gründet er die Albrecht-Graf-Goertz-Stiftung mit dem Ziel, junge Designer zu fördern.

Dort erlebte ich Graf Goertz 1993 bei einem Seminar, das wir für eine kleine Schar Designstudenten abhielten – ein grosses Erlebnis für mich. Er war ein Meister des Stils und erkannte sofort, wenn die Gestaltung keine Eleganz annahm. Für mich war er der 007 des Designs, der Gentleman-Designer, der bis zuletzt immer alleine arbeitete. Er war Vorbild, Legende, einfach ein großartiger Designer des letzten Jahrhunderts. Graf Goertz wird uns immer in den Gedanken bleiben.

already created the Paragon Coupé, his first independent design, an eye-catcher at the World Exhibition in San Francisco, which years later brought him the fateful acquaintance of the star designer Raymond Loewy, who recognised his talent and procured him a place to study design at the famous Pratt Institute in Brooklyn. Goertz worked as a Junior Designer in Loewy's Studebaker Development Department, and with Norman Bel Geddes, until in 1953 he set up his own firm in New York, called Goertz Industrial Design Inc.

One of the first major customers was Hohner, for whom he designed accordions and mouth-organs for the US market. But cars remained his first love. He made the acquaintance of Max Hoffmann, the most important American importer for luxury vehicles from overseas, who put him in touch with BMW. He designed the BMW 503 sports car, which was very well received. But in 1955 the BMW 507 was the big star of the Frankfurt Car Show, and Goertz was the new star in the design world's firmament. His name was now being mentioned in the same breath as greats like Pinin Farina, Bertone, and of course Raymond Loewy.

It was not only for the automotive sector that Goertz set new standards. He also designed office equipment and electrical appliances, cameras, radios and TV sets, plus furniture, jewellery and clothes. He was an interdisciplinary designer.

In 1989, at the age of 75, he returned to his old home, acting as an advisor to various firms and lecturing at universities.

In Brunkensen, he set up the Albrecht-Count-Goertz Foundation, with the aim of encouraging young designers. It was there that I met Count Goertz, at a seminar in 1993 that we held for a small group of design students, a deeply meaningful experience for me. He was a master of style, with a keen eye for any deficits in terms of elegance. For me, he was the 007 of the design world, the gentleman designer, who till the very end invariably worked alone. He was a role model, a legend, quite simply one of the last century's great designers. Count Goertz will always retain a special place in our memories.

DAS GUTE STÜCK

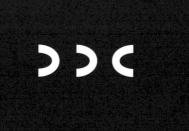

DAS GUTE STÜCK

GOLD

U-Bahnhof Lohring, Bochum

Aufgabe / Briefing: Konzeption, Entwurf, Werkplanung und künstlerische Oberleitung des Ausbaus der U-Bahnstation Lohring mit Zugangsebene, Verteilerebene und Mittelbahnsteigebene. **Umsetzung:** Die Elemente der Architektur – das Tunnelgewölbe, der gläserne Lichtboden, die mächtige rote Wand – verschmelzen mit dem Kunstkonzept aus Lichtlinien und Lichtkreuz und der Klanginstallation, die Geräusche des Ortes zu einem Klang-Environment formiert.

Auftraggeber / Client **Bochum-Gelsenkirchener Stadtbahn GbR** • Architektur / Architecture
RÜBSAMEN+PARTNER ARCHITEKTEN BDA INGENIEURE • Kunst & Musik / Art & Music
Eva-Maria Joeressen, Klaus Kessner

Assignment / Briefing: Conception, design, construction documentation and artistic supervision of the finishing work on the Lohring underground rail station with entry level, distribution level and island platform level. **Implementation:** The architectural elements – the tunnel vault, the luminous glass flooring, the massive red wall – merge with the artistic concept consisting of light lines and a luminous cross as well as with the acoustic installation, which makes an acoustic environment out of the sounds of the place.

Der Meissen ab 18 Kalender

Aufgabe / Briefing: Die Figuren von Meissen von ihrem Image als Staubfänger befreien und zeigen, dass sie noch immer Ausdruck zeitloser Kunst sind. **Umsetzung:** Entwicklung eines Kalenders, der die Figuren überraschend und modern inszeniert und so begehrenswert wie schöne Frauen darstellt.

Thema / Subject **Meissener Porzellan** • Auftraggeber / Client **Staatliche Porzellan-Manufaktur Meissen GmbH** • Designagentur / Designagency **Scholz & Friends, Berlin**

Assignment / Briefing: To support the sales of Meissen Porcelain figurines and fight their image as dust catchers - by proving that they are an expression of ageless art and beauty. **Implementation:** A calendar which shows the figurines in a surprisingly modern way, making them attractive as beautiful women in pin-up calendars.

Nonplusultra

Aufgabe / Briefing: Für den Wandkalender 2006 setzte Strichpunkt 150 Jahre alte Chromolithographien aus der Sammlung Kurt Weidemann hochwertig in Szene: ergänzt um zeitgemäßes Design in weiß auf weiß in diversen Veredelungstechniken präsentiert der Scheufelen Kalender das non plus ultra in der aktuellen Papiermacher-, Reproduktions- und Druckkunst.

Thema / Subject **Wandkalender 2006** • Auftraggeber / Client **Papierfabrik Scheufelen GmbH + Co. KG** • Designagentur / Designagency **Strichpunkt**

Assignment / Briefing: For its 2006 calendar, Strichpunkt uses 150-year-old chromolithographies from the Kurt Weidemann collection – and to tremendous effect: complemented by contemporary designs in white on white in various finishes, the Scheufelen calendar is the non plus ultra in state-of-the-art papermaking, reproduction and printing.

WIRKEN

Andrej Kupetz, Rat für Formgebung / German Design Council

www.german-design-council.de

ALcom Series

Aufgabe / Briefing: Gestaltung eines Möbelprogramms (Tisch- und Banksysteme), das den Raumsituationen neuer Architekturen gerecht wird. Leichtbau-Aluminiumpaneele (Wabenplatten) sind die tragenden Materialien. **Umsetzung:** Mit ihren Aluminiumpaneelen und höchster Detailgenauigkeit steht die klare, auf das Wesentliche reduzierte Geometrie der ALcom Tisch- und Banksysteme für eine architektonische Gestaltungsqualität.

Thema / Subject **Tisch- und Bankprogramm** • Auftraggeber / Client **ONE by ONE Co., Ltd.**
Designagentur / Designagency **f/p design gmbh**

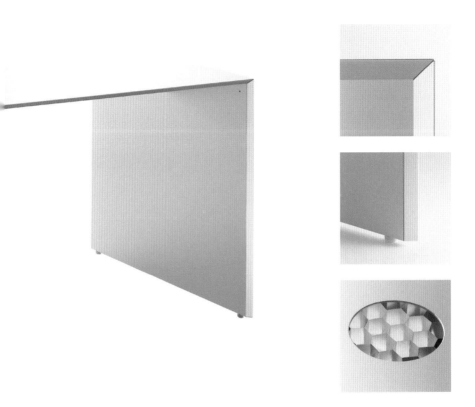

Assignment / Briefing: Design of a furniture range (desk and bench programs) in use of lightweight construction aluminium panels (honeycomb), meeting the space situations of new architectures.
Implementation: With its straight-line aluminium panels and its highest detail quality, the ALcom desk and bench series is reduced to the bare essentials and stands for a clear architectonic design quality.

SZ Krimi Bibliothek

Aufgabe / Briefing: Nachdem die Süddeutsche Zeitung die Bibliothek und die junge Bibliothek erfolgreich am Markt positionieren konnte, sollten Anfang 2006 die Krimifans auf ihre Kosten kommen. Die SZ Kriminalbibliothek beinhaltet die Klassiker des modernen Kriminalromans ebenso wie zahlreiche Geheimtipps und Wiederentdeckungen. **Umsetzung:** Die Kampagne setzt auf die Beobachtungsgabe und Kombinationsfreude der Krimi-Fans. Es wurde mit einer Bildsprache gearbeitet, die dem Betrachter erst bei genauerem Hinsehen das Thema näher bringt. Ob auf einer Yacht, einem herrschaftlichen englischen Landsitz oder einer niederländischen Windmühllandschaft. Auf den ersten Blick scheinen die Bilder einem Idyll entsprungen zu sein. Doch bei einem näheren Betrachten lässt sich neben der Headline erkennen, dass nichts ist, wie es scheint.

Thema / Subject **Bücherreihe mit Kriminalromanen einer Tageszeitung** • Auftraggeber / Client
Süddeutsche Zeitung GmbH • Designagentur / Designagency **GBK, Heye Werbeagentur GmbH**

Assignment / Briefing: After successfully establishing the "Library" and the "young Library" on the market, the "Sueddeutsche Zeitung" also wanted to please all fans of mystery novels. The SZ Criminal Library includes the classics of modern mystery novels as well as many sleepers and ediscoveries. **Implementation:** The campaign reckons on the power of observation and enjoyment of combination of criminal fans. The design reveals not before a very exact view, what the announcement is about. If on a yacht, a grand, english country seat or a Dutch mill landscape. On first sight the pictures seam to be a perfect idylle. But on a closer sight, not only the headline indicates, that nothing appears to be what it is.

Audi R8

Aufgabe / Briefing: Aufgabe war die Entwicklung einer Microsite zum Launch des Sportwagens von Audi, dem Audi R8. URL: http://www.audi.de/R8 **Umsetzung:** Besonders innovativ an der Microsite ist die zukunftsweisende Inszenierung des Audi R8 in Form eines interaktiven 3D-Films. Die Microsite startet mit einem Film, der den Audi R8 auf der Rennstrecke, in der Stadt und auf einer Küstenstraße zeigt. Jeder der 3D-gerenderten Filmsequenzen ist ein Kapitel zugeordnet: Innovation, Design und Performance. Zwischen den Sequenzen geht der Film jeweils in interaktive Zeitlupenszenen über, in denen der Nutzer Gelegenheit hat, Informationen zu den Themen aufzurufen. Der Audi R8 stoppt am Ende des Films in einem Hangar, wo den Nutzer eine drehbare 360-Grad-Ansicht mit Konfigurationsmöglichkeiten erwartet. Downloads wie Hintergrundbilder, Bildschirmschoner und Klingeltöne runden das Angebot ab.

DAS GUTE STÜCK

Thema / Subject **Audi R8** • Auftraggeber / Client **Audi AG** • Designagentur / Designagency **argonauten G2 GmbH**

Assignment / Briefing: The task involved developing a microsite to launch the Audi sports car, the Audi R8. URL: http://www.audi.de/R8. **Implementation:** The especially innovative aspect of the microsite is the pioneering representation of the Audi R8 in the form of an interactive 3-D film. The microsite starts with a film showing the Audi R8 on the racetrack, in the city and on a road along the coast. Each of the film sequences is assigned to a chapter. Innovation, Design and Performance. Interactive slow-motion scenes are inserted between these sequences, allowing the user to access information about the various topics. At the end of the film, the Audi R8 stops in a hangar, where the viewer is shown an adjustable 360° view with different configuration options. Downloads such as background images, screensavers and ringtones complete the site.

GOLD

"10 Jahre A&W-Designer-des-Jahres Cover"

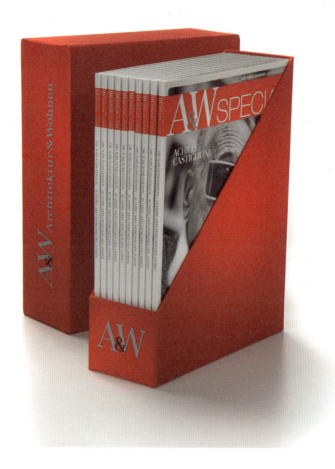

Aufgabe / Briefing: Um das Jubiläum „10 Jahre A&W-Designer-des-Jahres" gebührend in Szene zu setzen, entschied sich die Redaktion, dem aktuellen wie den ehemaligen Preisträgern jeweils eine Titelgestaltung des A&W-Specials zu widmen. **Umsetzung:** Die Titel mit den Portraits der 10 „A&W-Designern-des-Jahres" wurden bundesweit in Teilauflagen gestreut. Sammler können alle 10 Ausgaben ordern und erhalten einen Leinenschuber dazu.

Auftraggeber / Client **A&W Architektur&Wohnen**

Assignment / Briefing: To highlight the jubilee "10 Years of A&W-Designer-of-the-Year" condignly, the A&W-editorial office decided to dedicate an own cover design of the A&W-Special Edition to each, the current as well as to all the former laureates. **Implementation:** The issues with the several portraits of the 10 "A&W-Designers of the Year", were distributed in Germany in limited editions. Collectors can order all 10 issues and receive a linen-slipcase in addition.

DAS GUTE STÜCK

SILBER

Scharfe Messer

Aufgabe / Briefing: Einführung der GrandGourmet-Messer. **Umsetzung:** Die Messer sind so präzise und scharf, dass man selbst feinste Figuren aus dem Obst herausschneiden kann.

Thema / Subject **WMF GrandGourmet-Messer** • Auftraggeber / Client **WMF AG** • Designagentur / Designagency **KNSK**

Assignment / Briefing: Launching GrandGourmet kitchen knives **Implementation:** The knives are so sharp you can even create works of art out of fruit.

Planet Meer

Aufgabe / Briefing: Online-Kampagne für den neuen Bildband „Planet Meer" von National Geographic. Ziel ist es, die Marke online außergewöhnlich zu inszenieren und die Kunden mit sensationellen Unterwasseraufnahmen und Animationen selbst zum Entdecker werden zu lassen.
Umsetzung: Interaktives Flash-Special mit dem Ziel den Kunden durch sensationelle Unterwasseraufnahmen und Animationen selbst zum Entdecker werden zu lassen und die Markenwerte Faszination, Entdecken und Begeisterung online erlebbar zu machen. Tauchen Sie online!

Thema / Subject **Online-Kampagne für den Bildband „Planet Meer"** • Auftraggeber / Client
National Geographic Deutschland • Designagentur / Designagency **marke23 GmbH**

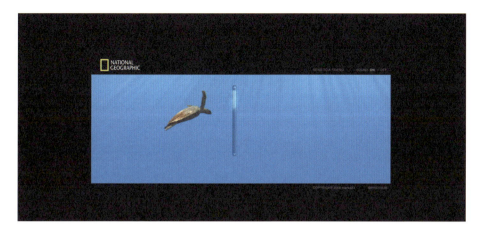

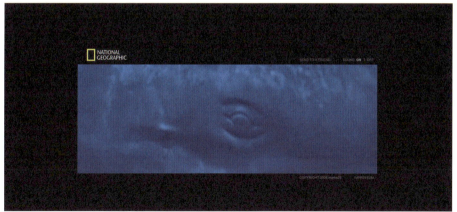

Assignment / Briefing: Development of an online Campaign for National Geographic's new illustrated book "Planet Meer". The aim is to allow the customer to become discoverers, with sensational underwater photographs and animations and thus stage the brand online, so that it can be experienced. **Implementation:** The aim of this interactive Flash-Special is to stage the brand values: fascination, discovery, enthusiasm online, so that it can be experienced by the client and to open up the brand through interactive dialogue. Dive online!

SILBER

Programmhefte Schauspiel Stuttgart

Thema / Subject **Programmhefte / programmes** • Auftraggeber / Client **Württembergische Staatstheater / Schauspiel Stuttgart** • Designagentur / Designagency **Strichpunkt**

Mercedes-Benz „PASSIONists"

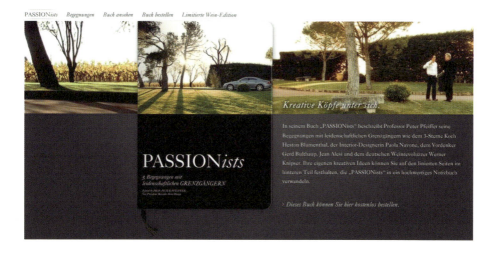

Aufgabe / Briefing: Der regelmäßige Dialog mit herausragenden Persönlichkeiten ist wichtige Inspiration für Mercedes-Chefdesigner Professor Peter Pfeiffer. Seine privaten Begegnungen mit Menschen wie Gerd Bulthaup, Jean Alesi und Werner Knipser hat er im Buch „PASSIONists" festgehalten. **Umsetzung:** Im zugehörigen Web-Special www.passionists.de kann „PASSIONists" exklusiv bestellt werden. Eingebettet in ein edles Seitendesign machen kurze Filme der Treffen Lust auf mehr. Ausgewählte Seiten des Buches kann der Anwender online durchblättern.

Auftraggeber / Client **DaimlerChrysler Vertriebsorganisation Deutschland**
Designagentur / Designagency **Elephant Seven AG**

Assignment / Briefing: The constant dialogue with outstanding personalities is an important inspiration for Mercedes chief designer Professor Peter Pfeiffer. His private meetings with design experts such as Gerd Bulthaup, Jean Alesi and Werner Knipser are documented in his book "PASSIONists".
Implementation: In the associated webspecial www.passionists.de, "PASSIONists" can be ordered exclusively online. Embedded in a precious design, the user gets inspired by watching short movies of the personal meetings and by reading selected pages of the book.

SILBER

www.hunderthundert.com

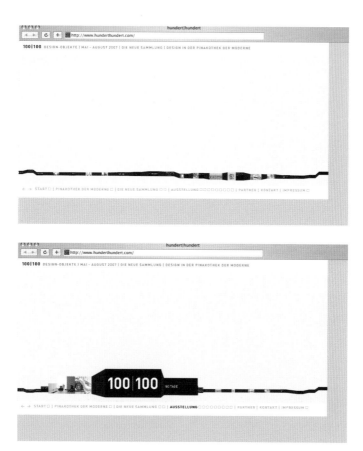

Aufgabe / Briefing: In der Ausstellung 100|100 werden hundert ausgewählte Objekte gezeigt, die das „Zeitalter des Designs" verkörpern. Die Exponate werden in einzelnen Metall-Cases ausgestellt, die zusammen ein fortlaufendes Band bilden, das sich diagonal über das Ausstellungsgelände erstreckt. **Umsetzung:** Für den Internetauftritt griffen wir die zugrunde liegende Idee auf: Ein horizontal fortlaufendes, bewegliches Band fungiert als Navigationsmenü, die einzelnen Inhalte sind darauf nacheinander abgebildet. Der Curser beeinflusst die Bewegung des Bandes, wird ein Inhalt ausgewählt, zoomt sich dieser Ausschnitt automatisch heran.

Thema / Subject **Internetauftritt** • Auftraggeber / Client **hundert|hundert GmbH**
Designagentur / Designagency **KMS**

Assignment / Briefing: The exhibition 100|100 displays one hundred select objects that embody the era of design. The exhibits are shown in individual metal cases which together form a continuous strip extending diagonally across the entire exhibition ground. **Implementation:** The website took up the underlying idea: A continuous horizontally moving strip functions as a navigational menu, displaying the contents in succession. The cursor controls the movement of the strip. When a particular content is selected, the view automatically zooms in on the relevant detail.

klima und mensch. leben in eXtremen

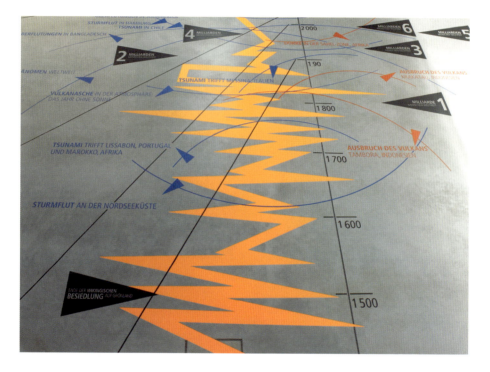

Aufgabe / Briefing: Was ist eigentlich Klima? Welche Auswirkungen hat es für das Leben auf der Erde und welchen Einfluss hat der Mensch? Häufen sich die Klimakatastrophen in der letzten Zeit oder gab es schon immer extreme Veränderungen? Die Ausstellung „klima und mensch. leben in eXtremen" gibt überraschende Antworten über die Anpassungsfähigkeit der Menschen, Tiere und Pflanzen über die Jahrtausende als auch über die Wetter-Extreme von vor sechs Millionen Jahren bis zu zukünftigen Hochwasserkatastrophen. **Umsetzung:** Entlang einer Klimakurve erlaubt die Inszenierung eine Zeit- und Entdeckungsreise und macht Themen wie Klimawandel, Entwicklung der Tier- und Pflanzenwelt und die Evolution des Menschen begeh- und erlebbar. Dabei bedient sich das Konzept klarer Informationsebenen die sich in eine mehrschichtige Landschaftsillusion eines in die Tiefe gestaffelten Raumbildes einfügen. Durch die geschickte, collagenartige Überlagerung von Realbild, Grafik, Text und Hintergrundmalerei und Exponaten entsteht eine Assoziation von landschaftlicher Entwicklung und dem Leben das sich dort abgespielt hat.

Thema / Subject **Temporäre Ausstellung im Westfälischen Museum für Archäologie Herne**
Auftraggeber / Client **Landschaftsverband Westfalen-Lippe** • Designagentur / Designagency
Atelier Brückner GmbH

Assignment / Briefing: What actually is climate? Which influences does the climate have on life on earth and which influence has the human? Do the climatic catastrophes recently accumulate or have there always been extremely changes? The concept of the exhibition seeks to imbue a broader public with an admiration for the adaptability and survivability of our ancestors who faced extreme changes in climate. **Implementation:** By walking along a climatic curve, the exhibition is arranged like an expedition, as a travel through time and space: themes and objects such as the development of flora and fauna, climate changes and the evolution of man become a walk through experience. The concept is structured in clear information levels, designed as a multilayered illusion of a landscape. By overlapping of real image, graphics, text, background painting and exhibits, an associativity on the development of landscape and life is formed.

SILBER

ISERLOHN – The Dornbracht Culture Projects, Vol.2

Aufgabe / Briefing: Die Dornbracht Armaturenfabrik unterstützt und initiiert seit 1996 kontinuierlich internationale Kulturprojekte und dokumentiert diese in Ausstellungskatalogen. Aufgabe war es, darüber hinaus ein Medium zu entwickeln, das aktuell an vergangene Projekte anknüpft und diese weiter thematisiert. **Umsetzung:** Die Publikation ist gleichzeitig Rückblick, Ausblick und Überblick über das komplexe kulturelle Engagement. Dokumentiert und porträtiert werden Künstler, Performances und Ausstellungen, die Dornbracht weltweit initiiert und inszeniert hat.

Thema / Subject **Kunst- und Kulturmagazin / Art and culture magazine** • Auftraggeber / Client **Aloys F. Dornbracht GmbH & Co. KG** • Designagentur / Designagency **Meiré und Meiré**

Assignment / Briefing: Dornbracht, the design fittings and accessories manufacturer has been sponsoring international culture projects continuously since 1996. The company has also made a point of documenting its cultural projects in exhibition catalogues. The task was also to develop a medium that would provide a modern link to past projects and continue to address them.
Implementation: This publication is a look back, a look forward and a summary of its complex cultural commitment. It documents and portrays international artists, performances and exhibitions staged and designed by Dornbracht.

POTT Kollektion / Collection 06

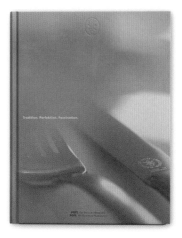

Aufgabe / Briefing: Die Neuinszenierung und -positionierung einer Traditionsmarke als Qualitätsmarktführer. **Umsetzung:** Ein Buch – für Fachhändler, Fachjournalisten, Architekten etc., das die Markenvision kommuniziert: POTT – Made in Germany – ist weltweit die Premiummarke für Bestecke. Manufakturfertigung und lebenslanger Service stehen für höchste Exklusivität.

Thema / Subject **Produktpräsentation** • Auftraggeber / Client **Seibel Designpartner GmbH**
Designagentur / Designagency **Buttgereit und Heidenreich GmbH**

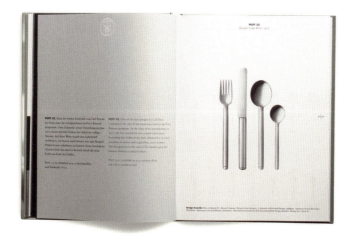

Assignment / Briefing: New staging and repositioning of a tradition brand as the quality market leader. **Implementation:** A book – for specialist dealers, specialised journalists, architects etc., that communicates the brand's vision: POTT – Made in Germany – is a premium brand for flatware worldwide. Handcrafted manufacturing and lifelong service represent ultimate exclusiveness.

SILBER

Mercedes-Benz Museum Stuttgart

Aufgabe / Briefing: HG Merz wurde bereits im Vorfeld des Architektenwettbewerbs als Kurator mit der inhaltlichen Konzeption des Museumsneubaus beauftragt und übernahm nach dessen Entscheidung die vollständige Planung und Ausführung des Ausstellungsdesigns. **Umsetzung:** Die Ausstellungsgestaltung, deren Konzeption auf der Analyse der umfangreichen Sammlung der Marke aufbaut, verfolgt ein narratives Konzept. Die Exponate sind die Stars und ihre Kontextualisierung steht im Vordergrund des Interesses.

Thema / Subject **Inhaltliche Konzeption des Museums, Gesamtkonzeption des musealen Ausbaus, Ausstellungsgestaltung** • Auftraggeber / Client **DaimlerChrysler Immobilien GmbH** Designagentur / Designagency **hg merz architekten museumsgestalter**

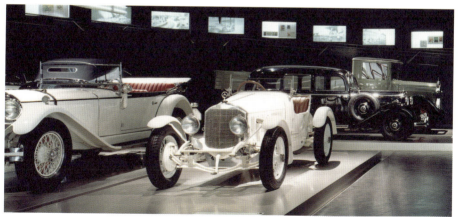

Assignment / Briefing: Already in the run-up to the architectural competition, HG Merz architectural practice was entrusted as curator, responsible for the concept of contents for the museum. After the competition's decision HG Merz was responsible for the complete planning and accomplishment of the exhibition design. **Implementation:** The exhibition design whose concept is based on the brand's large collection follows a narrative conception. Stars of the museum are the exhibits; the cars and their context are of main interest.

Leitsystem Kreissparkasse Tübingen

Aufgabe / Briefing: Entwicklung eines Orientierungssystems, das gleichzeitig auf den Glasflächen der transparenten Architektur als Gegenlaufschutz fungiert. **Umsetzung:** Der Schattenriss eines Baumes in Originalgröße belebt die Wände im Treppenhaus. In einem der oberen Geschosse scheinen Vögel, die auf die Glasfläche appliziert sind, umherzufliegen, ein Stockwerk tiefer sind es Schmetterlinge, darunter fallendes Laub und an einer aufgemalten Wiese erkennt man das Erdgeschoss.

Thema / Subject **Leitsystem** • Auftraggeber / Client **Kreissparkasse Tübingen**
Designagentur / Designagency **L2M3 Kommunikationsdesign GmbH**

Assignment / Briefing: Development of an orientation system on the glass surfaces of the transparent architecture, that also prevents movement in the wrong direction. **Implementation:** A life size tree silhouette livens up the walls in the staircase. In one of the top floors, birds that are applied to the glass surfaces seem to fly about; one floor below it's butterflies. Falling leaves indicate the first floor, and because of a painted meadow one recognizes the ground floor.

SILBER

Rosenbauer Panther

Aufgabe / Briefing: Neuentwicklung Flughafenlöschfahrzeug Rosenbauer Panther; Ausrichtung von Design und Technik auf die künftigen Anforderungen von Flughafenfeuerwehren; Schwerpunkte: Ergonomie, Dynamik, Sicherheit, moderne Werkstoffe, leistungsfähigste Löschtechnik. **Umsetzung:** Kraftvolle Formensprache betont die Attribute Verlässlichkeit, Sicherheit, Kraft und Dynamik; emotional ansprechendes Design unterstützt Position des Herstellers Rosenbauer als Weltmarktführer; Cockpit mit Rundum-Verglasung für besten Überblick.

Thema / Subject **Flughafenlöschfahrzeug** • Auftraggeber / Client **Rosenbauer International AG**
Designagentur / Designagency **Spirit Design / Innovation and Branding**

Assignment / Briefing: Redevelopment of airport fire engine Rosenbauer Panther; align design and engineering to airport fire brigades' future requirements; focus on ergonomics, dynamic, safety, modern materials, high performance fire-fighting systems. **Implementation:** Vigorous styling language stresses attributes such as reliability, safety, power and dynamism; emotionally appealing design supports Rosenbauer's position as world market leader; cab with panoramic windscreen made of safety glass for best overview.

SILBER

„Melting Pot. Stillleben mit Blumen"

Aufgabe / Briefing: Die Floristin Carola Wineberger wurde beauftragt, Wintersträuße zu kreieren, die unkonventionell sind, schlicht, aber besonders. **Umsetzung:** Wineberger wählte Pflanzen der Jahreszeit und kombinierte sie originell – in Vasen ebenso wie in einfachen Wassergläsern. Als Kulisse wurden triviale Locations genutzt, die in Kontrast zur Poesie der Sträuße stehen – und sie dadurch „erhöhen".

Auftraggeber / Client **A&W Architektur&Wohnen**
Designagentur / Designagency **A&W Architektur&Wohnen**

Assignment / Briefing: The florist Carola Wineberger was commissioned to create bouquets for the winter that are unconventional and simple but experimental the same way. **Implementation:** Wineberger chose seasonable plants and combined them in a fancy way – in vases as well as in water glasses. The settings were trivial locations in contrast to the poetry of the bouquets, which thereby were enhanced.

FEINSTE PAPIERE SIND UNSERE

PASSION. Ingo Wolfarth, RÖMERTURM Feinstpapier

www.roemerturm.de

FORM:ETHIK Ein Brevier für Gestalter

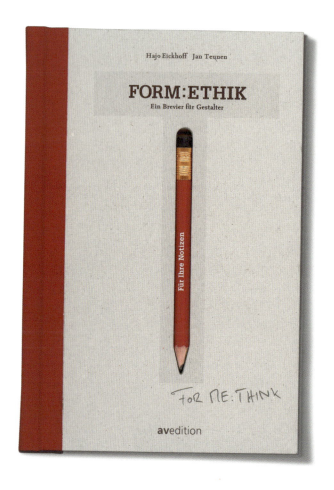

Aufgabe / Briefing: Das „Brevier für Gestalter" versteht sich als Arbeitsbuch, das zur Auseinandersetzung, zum Austausch und Dialog anstiften will. Arbeitsinstrumente – Bleistift, Dialogkarten und Blanko-Seiten für eigene Gedanken liefert es gleich mit. Der Satzspiegel wurde als Prägung hinterlegt, um die persönlichen Anmerkungen, die nach und nach die Blanko-Seiten füllen werden ins Buch zu integrieren und ihren Wert zu unterstreichen.

Auftraggeber / Client **designafairs** • Designagentur / Designagency **KOCHAN & PARTNER GmbH, München**

Assignment / Briefing: The "Designer's Breviary" shall be understood as a workbook which wants to encourage discussion, exchange and dialogue. Working tools – pencil, dialogue cards and blank-pages for own thoughts are enclosed right away. The print space has been marked with an embossment to underline the value of the private anotations, which will fill the blank pages by and by.

Deftige Deutschlandreise

Aufgabe / Briefing: Traditionelle, regionale Rezepte mit einer Story zu präsentieren. **Umsetzung:** Sechs deutsche Gerichte wurden in dieser Food-Strecke als eine nostalgische Reise in Szene gesetzt. Fotografie, Styling und Requisite stellen den Bezug zu Herkunft und Tradition des jeweiligen Rezepts her. Räume und Gegenstände erscheinen in gedämpftem Licht und gedeckten Tönen. Fokus und Farbigkeit liegen auf dem Food.

Auftraggeber / Client **COUNTRY**

Assignment / Briefing: Presenting traditional, local recipes in a story. **Implementation:** Six German dishes are staged as a nostalgic journey in this picture gallery. Photography, styling and prop built the relation to the origin and to the tradition of each recipe. Rooms and objects appear in cushioned light and muted tones. The focus is on the coloured food.

Rettung für das Rote Mangalitza

Aufgabe / Briefing: Die alten, vom Aussterben bedrohten Nutztierrassen der Arche Warder interessant zu präsentieren. **Umsetzung:** Die Fotos, die mit Bilderrahmen und Namensschildern versehen sind, portraitieren die Tiere wie in einer Ahnengalerie und heben ihre spezifischen Eigenarten hervor. Ungerahmte Fotos beim Text am Ende der Strecke illustrieren ihren Lebensraum – so sind die zwei Ebenen der Geschichte optisch betont.

Auftraggeber / Client **COUNTRY**

Assignment / Briefing: Presenting the old and endangered races of Arche Warder's farm animals in an interesting way. **Implementation:** The prints with picture frames and name plates portrait the animals like an ancestral portrait gallery and accent their specific characters. Unframed pictures in the end illustrate their habitat – that is how the two levels of the story are optically stressed.

FORM IST INHALT

Gerrit Terstiege, Chefredakteur der Zeitschrift form

www.form.de

SILBER

ONGWE – Der Leopard

Aufgabe / Briefing: Der Bildband Ongwe ist ein Gemeinschaftsprojekt von Thomas Kettner und kpg Design. Mit dem Bildband soll auf das Volk der Himba aufmerksam gemacht werden, das der zunehmenden Bedrohung durch unkontrollierten Tourismus und den Erschließungsplänen der Namibischen Regierung ausgesetzt ist. Die Erlöse des Projekts kommen einem noch einzurichtenden Fonds in Namibia zugute, der es den Himba ermöglichen soll, ihre ethnischen und juristischen Interessen vor der Regierung Namibias zu vertreten. **Umsetzung:** Die Vorzugsausgabe des Bildbandes ist mit einer mächtigen Lederhülle umschlagen. In einem Mix aus Inszenierung und spontaner / reportageartiger Fotografie entfaltet sich die Geschichte einer Journalistin, die ins Herz Afrikas reist, wo ihre Erfahrungen und Sehnsüchte mit dem Alltag eines traditionellen Hirtenvolks kollidieren. Kraftvolle Bilder in erdigen Farben wechseln sich mit großzügiger Typografie ab.

Thema / Subject **Buch / Bildband** • Auftraggeber / Client **Thomas Kettner**
Designagentur / Designagency **kpg Grafikdesign, Täferrot**

Assignment / Briefing: The picturebook ONGWE is a united project of Thomas Kettner and kpg Design. The object of this book was to draw attention to the HIMBA tribe in northern Namibia, who are severely endangered of getting extinct, due to uncontrolled tourism and plans of the Namibian government to build a huge hydro electric powerplant. The money retrieved from this project, after paying for the costs, would be donated to a trust fund, still to be emplaced. The money is to support the ethnical interest of the tribe. **Implementation:** The limited edition of the book has a mighty leather-cover. A mix of spontane / journalistic and staged photography tells the story of a female journalist, travelling through the heart of Africa, where her experience and yearning clashes with the day to day life of the traditional HIMBA tribe. Emotional pictures in earthy tones alternate with unstinting typography.

BRONZE

BRONZE

Dieter Blum: nice pair/Cattedrale del Corpo/pure dance

Aufgabe / Briefing: Gestaltung eines Ausstellungskatalog für Dieter Blum's Fotografien auf der Tanzbiennale in Venedig 2005. Der Katalog sollte kombiniert werden mit dem bereits veröffentlichten Buch - pure dance - von Dieter Blum. **Umsetzung:** Die Grundgestaltung von – pure dance – wurden für den Ausstellungskatalog adaptiert und um eine aggressive Farbe erweitert: neonrot. Diese Farbe transportiert die Aktualität des Katalogs, ohne die zurückhaltende Eleganz von – pure dance – zu stören. Ein Schuber dient als Klammer und Behältnis. Eine neonrote Banderole umschließt das Set und gibt ihm den Namen: a nice pair.

Thema / Subject **Ausstellungskatalog Biennale Venedig 2006** • Auftraggeber / Client **Biennale Venedig, Direktor Ismael Ivo**

Assignment / Briefing: To design an exhibition catalog for Dieter Blum's photographs as were showcased at the Venice Dance Biennial in 2005. The catalog was to be combined with – pure dance – Dieter Blum's book of dance photos, which was already on the market. **Implementation:** The underlying design of – pure dance – was adapted for the exhibition catalog and expanded to include an aggressive color, namely neon red. This color aptly conveys the topical nature of the catalog without disturbing the restrained elegance of – pure dance –. The box for the set doubles up as an motif and framing context. The neon red paper band completes the set and gives it the appropriate name – a nice pair.

Lichtsinfonie Berliner Hauptbahnhof

Aufgabe / Briefing: Schaffung von Awareness und Akzeptanz durch Inszenierung von Architektur, Botschaften und Historie als multimediales Gesamtkunstwerk „Lichtsinfonie" unter Einbindung eines renommierten Lichtkünstlers. **Umsetzung:** Um den Bahnhof und die Deutsche Bahn optimal darzustellen, wurde die Sinfonie mit Musik und Licht inszeniert. Sie wurde unterstützt durch Pyrotechnik, Projektionen und Laser.

Thema / Subject **Lichtsinfonie** • Auftraggeber / Client **Deutsche Bahn Station und Service AG**
Designagentur / Designagency **Scholz & Friends Brand Affairs GmbH**

Assignment / Briefing: Creation of awareness and acceptance through staging architecture, messages and history as a multimedia work of art, called "Symphony of light", under the engagement of a well-known lighting artist. **Implementation:** To present the central station and the Deutsche Bahn optimally, the symphony was staged by using music and light. It was supported by the use of pyrotechnics, projections and laser.

Kaffeeschlange

Aufgabe / Briefing: Trilicious ist eine Pre-Processed Food Marke im oberen Preissegment. Unter der Bezeichnung „Premium Frozen Sandwiches" werden tief gefrorene Produkte angeboten, die für den Verzehr im Kontaktgrill erhitzt werden. Als Diversifikation kam 2005 eine Kaffeemarke hinzu. Um den Gedanken der Dachmarke Trilicious – Schnelligkeit und Convenience in Verbindung mit hoher Produktqualität und Genuss – auch für das Produkt Kaffee erlebbar zu machen, entwickelten wir einen Getränkeautomaten der ganz besonderen Art. **Umsetzung:** Die Trilicious-Kaffeeschlange ist ein Getränkeautomat und Gaststätte in einem. Sie verbindet Design, Technik und sozialen Ort auf kleinstem Raum.

Thema / Subject **Trilicious Kaffeeschlange** • Auftraggeber / Client **Trilicious GmbH**
Designagentur / Designagency **Schitto Schmodde Waack Werbeagentur GmbH**

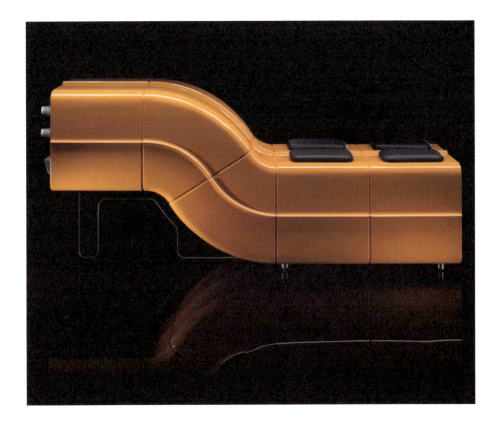

Assignment / Briefing: Trilicious is a pre-processed food brand in the upper price segment. Main products are "Premium Frozen Sandwiches" which are cooked to order. As a diversification a coffee brand was added in 2005. To allow the idea of the branded-house Trilicious – quickness and convenience paired with high quality products and enjoyment – to be experienced through the coffee product as well, we developed a very special "coffee maker". **Implementation:** The Trilicious Coffee Snake combines a vending machine with a Coffeehouse. It connects design, engineering and a social spot within a minimum of space.

Read. Grow.

Aufgabe / Briefing: Steigerung des Bekanntheitsgrades in der Zielgruppe der Top-Entscheider.
Umsetzung: „Capital" ist der Ratgeber für den beruflichen Aufstieg.

Auftraggeber / Client **Gruner & Jahr (Capital)** • Designagentur / Designagency **KNSK, Werbeagentur GmbH**

Assignment / Briefing: Increasing brand awareness within the target group of top decision makers.
Implementation: "Capital" is the guidebook for professional advancement.

BRONZE

PRO-SAFE™-Themendarstellung Mercedes-Benz IAA 2005

Aufgabe / Briefing: Themendarstellung der integrierten Sicherheitsphilosophie PRO-SAFE™ von Mercedes-Benz für den Ersteinsatz auf der IAA 2005. PRO-SAFE™ gliedert sich in vier Phasen, die sich an möglichen Unfallszenarien orientieren. Die einzelnen Phasen mit den entsprechenden Sicherheitsfeatures sowie der übergreifende Sicherheitsgedanke sollen auf der IAA 2005 räumlich spürbar werden: in einem für die Besucher erfahr- und erlebbaren „Sicherheitskörper".

Thema / Subject **Begehbarer SicherheitsraumBenz IAA 2005** • Auftraggeber / Client **Daimler-Chrysler AG** • Designagentur / Designagency **Atelier Markgraph (AM) und Entwurfswerk (EW)**

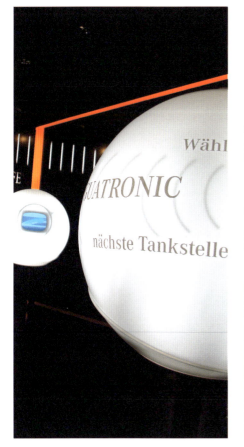

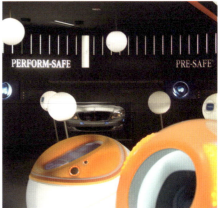

Assignment / Briefing: A topical overview of the integrated PRO-SAFE™ safety philosophy invented by Mercedes-Benz and shown for the first time at the IAA 2005. PRO-SAFE™ consists of four phases to address possible accident scenarios. Each individual phase with its unique safety features as well as the overall safety concept are intended to be a physical experience: every visitor is given the chance to feel and experience a "safety body".

BRONZE

Fahrradweg

Aufgabe / Briefing: Steppenwolf soll als kompetenter Hersteller von hochwertigen Mountainbikes dargestellt werden, deren Material und Qualität höchsten Ansprüchen genügt. **Umsetzung:** Anstatt mit der Beschreibung technischer Features zu werben, konzentriert sich die Idee auf das eigentlich Wichtige, den Ort, wo Bikerträume wahr werden. Durch die Ergänzung eines Fahrradweg-Schildes in eine raue Naturlandschaft, wird die Aussage getroffen: Hier (und auch sonst überall) kannst Du mit Steppenwolf Mountain Bikes hin.

Assignment / Briefing: To build up a general reputation for Steppenwolf quality mountain bikes. **Implementation:** Instead of explaining technical features, the idea focuses on the really important things – the places, where biker-dreams become reality. By dropping a bike-lane sign onto a picture of a rough nature landscape, we tell the customer: You can go there (and anywhere else you want to) with Steppenwolf mountain bikes.

Auftraggeber / Client **Steppenwolf GmbH** • Designagentur / Designagency **Heye & Partner GmbH**

BRONZE

Internetpräsenz des Zukunftcamps der Deutschen Telekom AG

Aufgabe / Briefing: 13-jährige Kinder als Hauptakteure eines Kongresses – das ist die Idee des Zukunftscamps der Deutschen Telekom. Die Website soll das zentrale, zielgruppenadäquate Medium zur Vorbereitung und Begleitung des Großevents sein. **Umsetzung:** Die Workshop-Themen wurden spielerisch aufbereitet. Viele innovative Features wie die Videoreportagen von Kindern für Kinder, Online-Spiele, Live-Streams und virtuelle Post-its animierten zahlreiche Kinder zur Teilnahme.

Auftraggeber / Client **Deutsche Telekom AG**
Designagentur / Designagency **people interactive GmbH**

Assignment / Briefing: The idea behind the "future camp" presented by the Deutsche Telekom is a convention for 13 year old children. The website is to be the central medium for preparation and accompaniment of the event adapted to the young target group. **Implementation:** The workshop topics were put into a playful, hands-on context. Many innovative features such as video reportages from kids for kids, online games, live streams and virtual post-its incited many children to participate.

Coke Datenvisualisierung

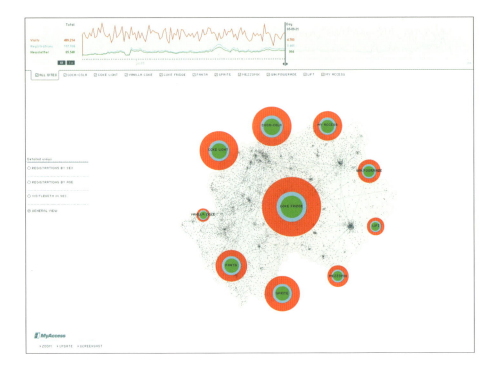

Aufgabe / Briefing: Ziel des Online-Tools ist die Visualisierung des Nutzerverhaltens auf den Coca-Cola Markenwebsites. Für Controlling und Marketingverantwortliche bei Coca-Cola dient das Tool der Steigerung von Effektivität und Effizienz von Online-Marketingmaßnahmen. **Umsetzung:** Die Applikation zeigt auf einem Screen die Anzahl, Verbreitung und Aktivität der User in Deutschland im zeitlichen Ablauf. Die Informationen stammen aus verschiedenen Web-Statistiken und Customer Relations-Datenbanken, deren komplexe Zusammenhänge nachvollziehbar dargestellt und analysiert werden können.

Thema / Subject **Datenvisualisierung** • Auftraggeber / Client **Coca-Cola GmbH**
Designagentur / Designagency **Scholz & Volkmer**

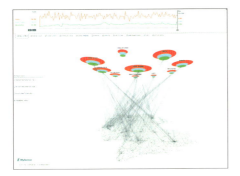
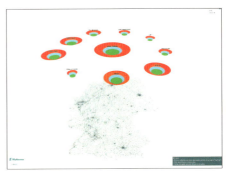
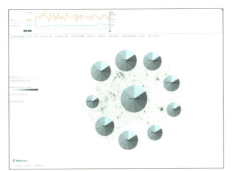
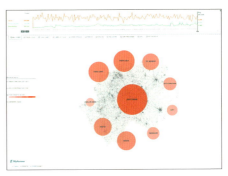

Assignment / Briefing: Objective of the online tool is to visualise user behaviour on the different brand websites of Coca-Cola. Added value for Controlling and Marketing by increasing the effectiveness and efficiency of online marketing activities. **Implementation:** The application displays the visits, registrations and activities of users in Germany. The data come from diverse logfile-tables and customer relations databases, whose complex interrelationships are presented on only one screen in a clear and understandable manner.

BRONZE

Mercedes-Benz E-Klasse Experience Paris-Peking

Aufgabe / Briefing: Zur Einführung der neuen Mercedes-Benz E-Klasse-Generation starten 33 E-Klasse Modelle am 21. Oktober 2006 auf eine Langstreckenfahrt von Paris nach Peking. Ziel des Webspecials ist es, die unterschiedlichen Phasen der Experience (Bewerbung, Vorberichterstattung, Live Coverage und Nachberichterstattung) zu begleiten und für den User erlebbar zu machen.
Umsetzung: Eine interaktive Google Maps-Anwendung wird auf Mercedes-Benz.com integriert und ermöglicht es den Usern, die Route zu erkunden und die Position der Fahrzeuge in Echtzeit mitzuverfolgen. Die unterschiedlichen Phasen der Experience werden durch einen virtuellen Tourmoderator und Liveschaltungen begleitet.

DAS GUTE STÜCK

Auftraggeber / Client **DaimlerChrysler AG** • Designagentur / Designagency **Scholz & Volkmer**

Assignment / Briefing: On October 21st 2006, 33 Mercedes-Benz E-Class models will be going on their long-distance journey from Paris to Peking. Goal of the webspecial is to accompany the different phases (application, pre-coverage, live coverage and post-coverage) and enable the users to experience the journey by themselves. **Implementation:** An interactive Google Maps application will be integrated into the Mercedes-Benz website making it possible for users to explore the route and to follow the current locations of the vehicles in realtime. The different phases of the journey are accompanied by a virtual tour host and live broadcasts to the drivers.

Gesammelte Helden
Die Fußballweltmeister von 1974 – und in uns glühen die Erinnerungen ...

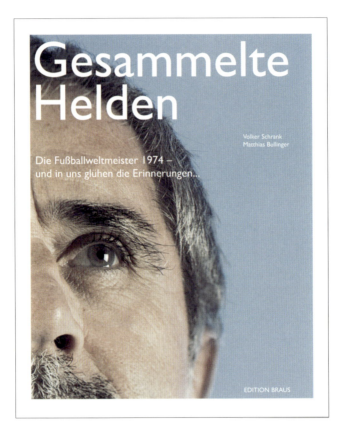

Aufgabe / Briefing: Mit seiner Porträtserie thematisiert Volker Schrank den Prozess der medialen Konstruktion des Helden, der Entstehung eines Mythos. Die Texte behandeln die politische Situation während der Fußball-WM 1974, den Mythos von Weltmeistern, die Leidenschaft des Sammelns, den Zeitgeist und nicht zuletzt: den Fußball selbst. **Umsetzung:** Die Helden der Fußball-WM 1974 sollen so abgebildet werden, dass sie – herausgelöst aus dem bekannten Wahrnehmungskontext – dem Betrachter vertraut und fremd zugleich erscheinen. Entrückt und überlebensgroß stehen sie für den Mythos, den sie als Helden des Fussballs im kollektiven Gedächtnis über ihre Generation hinaus verkörpern.

Thema / Subject **Buch** • Auftraggeber / Client **Edition Braus im Wachter Verlag**
Designagentur / Designagency **bildkultur**

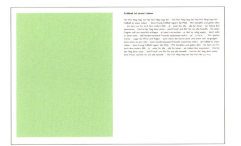

Assignment / Briefing: In this series of portraits, Volker Schrank turns the process of how a hero is constructed in the media into this topic: the creation of a German myth. The essays reflect the political situation in Germany during the 1974 World Championship 1974, the myths about world champions, the passion of collectors and foremost: soccer itself. **Implementation:** Volker Schrank depicts the players of the 1974 World champion squad removing them frome of the tradional perceptional context: for the observer at the same time familiar and unusual. Entranced and taller than life, the squad members of the 1974 German World Championship team stand for the myth, which they embody as footballing heroes in the collective memory beyond their own generation.

ERFOLG IST BEHARRLICHE
ORIENTIERUNG AN

Hartmut Preis, Druckwerkstätten Dieter Hoffmann

)ER QUALITÄT

www.druckerei-hoffman.de

Armin Lindauer: Helmut Lortz – leicht sinnig

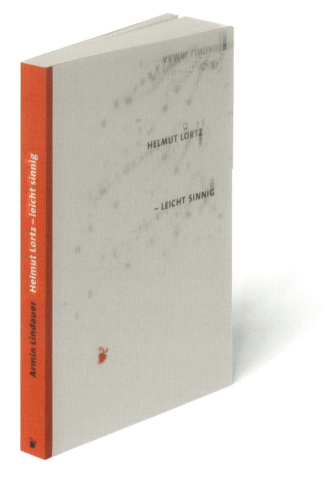

Aufgabe / Briefing: Gedichte, Aphorismen und kurze Texte von Helmut Lortz sollen in einem Buch publiziert werden. **Umsetzung:** Den Texten wurden Zeichnungen, die auch von Helmut Lortz stammen, gegenübergestellt und typografisch inszeniert. Das Leichte und Spielerische, das Melancholische und Ernsthafte der Texte soll in der Gestaltung, von der Typografie, über die Flexibilität des Buches, bis zur Titelgestaltung (Wackelbild) ihre Entsprechung finden..

Thema / Subject **Buch** • Auftraggeber / Client **Stadt Darmstadt**

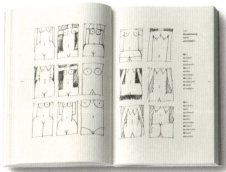

Assignment / Briefing: Poems, aphorisms and short texts by Helmut Lortz are to be published in a book. **Implementation:** Texts by Helmut Lortz were set alongside a number of his own drawings and staged typografically. The light and playful character of the texts, their melancholy and seriousness is meant to appear in the design of the book as well, starting with typography and the flexibility of the book, right up to the cover design, which features a type of wobbly picture otherwise used for fun postcards.

BRONZE

WECHSELRAUM Bund Deutscher Architekten, Corporate Design

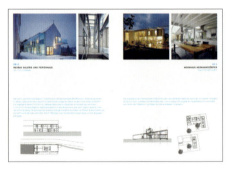

Aufgabe / Briefing: Der Wechselraum ist transformierbarer Galerieraum und Treffpunkt für die Architekturszene in Stuttgart, in dem Diskussionen, Vorträge und Ausstellungen stattfinden – eine Plattform für Architektur. Insbesondere die Gestaltung der Plakate und Ausstellungskataloge sollte trotz verschiedenster Inhalte als durchgehende, einprägsame Reihe funktionieren. **Umsetzung:** Die klare, markante Raumgeometrie stand Pate für das Gestaltungskonzept des Erscheinungsbilds. Der abstrahierte Grundriss des Raumes bildet ein robustes Raster für die Gestaltung aller Kommunikationsmedien – der Grundriss wird zum überdimensionalen Signet. Dieses Raster funktioniert als eine Art Container in der Gestaltung der Medien für alle Ausstellungen und Veranstaltungen. Die Print-Publikationen und die Typografie spielen mit der Haptik und Optik des Ausstellungsraums – raue und glatte, matte und glänzende Oberflächen, verschiedene Grautöne und starke Kontraste. Die Typografie ist klar und entschieden. Das Gestaltungskonzept der Ausstellungen, als horizontales Tapetenband angedacht, fließt konsequent in Form von 8-seitigen Umschlägen der Print-Publikationen und auf der Website durch die horizontale Anordnung der Inhalte ein.

Thema / Subject **Corporate Design** • Auftraggeber / Client **Bund Deutscher Architekten, Baden-Württemberg** • Designagentur / Designagency **ippolito fleitz group**

Assignment / Briefing: The Wechselraum is a transformable gallery and meeting point for Stuttgart's architectural scene which is open for discussions, lectures and extraordinary exhibitions in the context of architecture. The aim was to position the Wechselraum as a platform for architecture. Because of the heterogeneity of the expected contents the design had to be clear, robust and brand recognisable. **Implementation:** The graphic appearance was modelled on the significant and clear actual space. The abstract floor plan forms a robust grid for designing all communication means – the plan forms an oversized signet. This grid functions as a type of container for designing all media related to exhibitions and events. The printed matter play with haptics and optics of the Wechselraum interior design – rough and smooth, mat and glossy surfaces, shades of grey and high contrasts. The typography is clear and determined. The design approach of the exhibitions as a horizontal wallpaper band is used consequently by 8-sided jackets for the printed matter and by horizontal arrangement of the information on the website.

BRONZE

„Einblicke – Mercedes-Benz Museum"

Aufgabe / Briefing: Im Mai 2006 öffnete das neue Mercedes-Benz Museum seine Pforten. Ein Museumsprojekt der Superlative! Die Wanderausstellung „Einblicke" soll die Besucher neugierig machen und einstimmen auf die große Schau. **Umsetzung:** Facsimile, kuriose Gegenstände und interessante Geschichten aus der rund 120-jährigen Geschichte der Automarke finden sich in sieben Archivboxen. Die Ausstellungsidee setzt auf die Neugier der Besucher zu entdecken, was in den Boxen steckt. Komplettiert wird die Ausstellung durch eine Infowand mit Fakten und einem Film zum neuen Museum.

Thema / Subject **Wanderausstellung** • Auftraggeber / Client **DaimlerChrysler AG**
Designagentur / Designagency **design hoch drei GmbH & Co.KG**

Assignment / Briefing: The new Mercedes-Benz museum opened its doors in May 2006. And it's a superlative project! The travelling exhibition A peak behind the Scenes aims at making visitors curious and getting them in the right frame of mind for the big event. **Implementation:** Facsimile, odd objects and interesting stories of the car manufacturer's approximately 120 years of corporate history have been stored in seven archive boxes. The exhibition bets on the visitor's curiosity to discover what's in the boxes. A noticeboard and a film introducing the new museum complement the exhibition.

BRONZE

Das Wissen der Welt

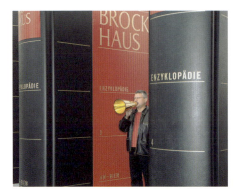

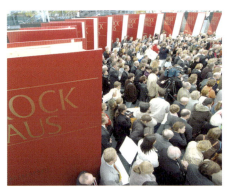

Aufgabe / Briefing: Inszenierung des 200 jährigen Jubiläums von Brockhaus und der neuen Brockhaus-Ausgabe auf der Buchmesse Frankfurt. Kreation eines Pressemotivs. **Umsetzung:** Installation von 30 dreieinhalb Meter großen Brockhaus-Bänden, die in einem weiten Kreis aufgestellt waren. Zu verstehen war dies als Hommage an die zeitlose Gültigkeit des Wissens in den Enzyklopädien von Brockhaus. Der Kreis konnte von allen Seiten betreten werden. Dazu drang eine permanente Klangperformance aus den verschiedenen Bänden ans Ohr des Besuchers: Das Wissen der Welt wurde hör- und greifbar. Eigens für das Enthüllungsevent wandelte sich der Buchkreis zur Bühne für eine Sprechoper, wobei die Künstler solo und im Chor singend durch die Installation schritten, bevor ihre Stimmen im Finale von oben aus den Büchern heraus tönten.

Thema / Subject **Messe-Inzenierung** • Auftraggeber / Client **Bibliographisches Institut & F.A. Brockhaus AG Baden-Württemberg** • Designagentur / Designagency **Milla und Partner Agentur & Ateliers**

Assignment / Briefing: Creation of a unique experience and press motiv for press, public and booksellers on the occasion of the 200th anniversary of Brockhaus and the launch of the 21st edition at the book fair in Frankfurt October 2005. **Implementation:** The installation of 30 replicas of the Brockhaus Encyclopedia - each of them 3,40m high - placed in a round formation was a tribute to the timeless validity of the knowledge in the encyclopedias of Brockhaus. The circle of enormous books could be entered from all sides. In addition, a permanent sound performance could be heard from each of the different volumes: the knowledge of the world became audible. For the unveiling of the installation, a phonetic opera for 30 + 1 voices was composed and performed, with the choir standing high above the audience in the Brockhaus-replicas, and the soloist in the middle of the circle.

BRONZE

Gira Light & Building 2006

Aufgabe / Briefing: Entwurf & Realisation eines Messestandes für die Light & Building 2006 in Frankfurt. Das Thema der Messe „Light & Building" wird zum Programm der Präsentation.
Umsetzung: In einer speziell entwickelten Glastragwerkkonstruktion sind Leuchtstoffröhren montiert, die aus dem Glaskubus insgesamt einen überdimensionalen, taghellen Leuchtkörper machen. bevor ihre Stimmen im Finale von oben aus den Büchern heraus tönten.

Thema / Subject **Messestand** • Auftraggeber / Client **Gira Giersiepen GmbH & Co KG**
Designagentur / Designagency **Schmitz visuelle Kommunikation**

Assignment / Briefing: Design & Realisation of a stand for the Light & Building 2006 in Frankfurt. The subject of the exhibition "Light & Building" becomes the program of the presentation.
Implementation: Fluorescent tubes are installed in a special glass girder construction which overall form the glass cube into an over dimensional, daylight illuminant.

BRONZE

Audi Markenbuch – Vorsprung durch Technik

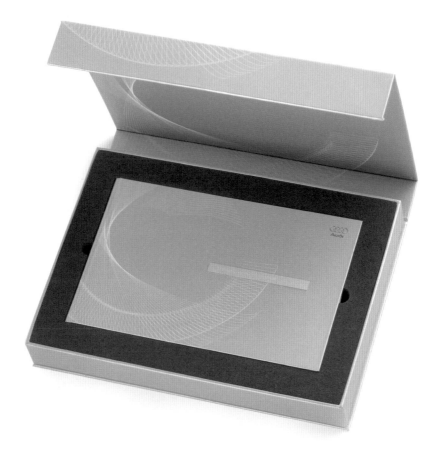

Aufgabe / Briefing: Erstellung eines Markenbuches für Führungskräfte der Audi AG als inhaltlicher und emotionaler Leitfaden für (Selbst-) Verständnis und Wertevermittlung der Marke Audi. Grundlage ist die Premiumstrategie der Marke für die nächsten 10 Jahre. **Umsetzung:** Haltung, keine Unterhaltung – nach diesem Credo stellt das Audi Markenbuch die Essenz von Audi plastisch dar. Dies tut es auf prägnante, klare und zugleich emotionale Weise, ohne effekthascherisch sein zu wollen. Vorsprung muss zunächst im Kopf entstehen.

Thema / Subject **Markenbuch / Automobil** • Auftraggeber / Client **Audi AG**
Designagentur / Designagency **Mutabor Design GmbH**

Assignment / Briefing: To create a brand book for Audi AG's senior managers and other executives as a guideline, both content-related and emotional, on how to understand the Audi brand (and themselves) and communicate its values to the outside world. The basis is provided by the brand's premium strategy for the next 10 years. **Implementation:** Attitude, not entertainment – this is the credo according to which the Audi brand book vividly presents the essence of Audi. It does this concisely, clearly and the same time emotionally, without any cheap showmanship. 'Vorsprung' must first take place in the mind.

KUNST|RAD – Museumsuferfest Frankfurt 2005

Aufgabe / Briefing: Schaffung eines großen Zeichens für das Thema des Museumsuferfestes 2005: „Die Welt der Kultur | Die Kultur der Welt" und Stärkung des öffentlichen Bewusstseins für Frankfurts Kulturreichtum. **Umsetzung:** Ein Riesenrad wird zur Bühne für die Museen. Das KUNST | RAD bringt 100 Meisterwerke aus 16 Häusern am Main auf die große Leinwand. Dabei steht jede Gondel für ein Museum. Die Inszenierung verbindet romantischen Jahrmarkt und Großstadtkulisse mit modernster Medientechnik: Der Takt der Bespielung wird über Sensoren am Rad vom Besucherstrom selbst bestimmt.

Thema / Subject **Licht- und Medieninszenierung** • Auftraggeber / Client **Tourismus+Congress GmbH Frankfurt am Main** • Designagentur / Designagency **Atelier Markgraph GmbH**

Assignment / Briefing: Create a large symbol for the motto of the 2005 Museum Riverbank Festival: "World Culture | Cultural World", and heighten the public awareness of Frankfurt's cultural treasures.
Implementation: A Ferris Wheel becomes a stage for the museums. ART | WHEEL brings international masterpieces from 16 Frankfurt museums out onto the big screen. Each museum has its own gondola. ART | WHEEL is a magical mix of fairground romance, city skyline and modern media: The visitors themselves determine the projection's rhythm, thanks to sensors in the wheel.

Modernisierung on Tour

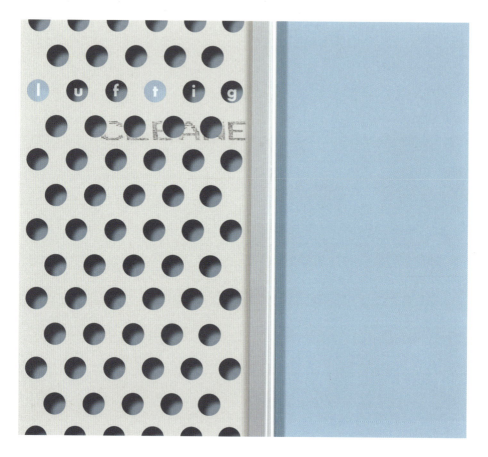

Aufgabe / Briefing: Entwicklung von 6 Exponaten für die Wanderausstellung „Modernisierung on Tour". Die Exponate sollen dem Fachhandel die Vorteile der Knauf Produkte kurzweilig vermitteln. Aus Kostengründen muss der Aufbau der Exponate von einer Person innerhalb von 4 Stunden durchgeführt werden können. **Umsetzung:** Jedes Exponat ermöglicht die interaktive Auseinandersetzung und fördert dadurch die selbst erlebte Wahrnehmung der fokussierten Produktvorteile. Das Produkt an sich wird zum musealen Objekt und dokumentiert ganz selbstverständlich die Symbiose aus Funktionalität und Ästhetik.

Thema / Subject **Exponate** • Auftraggeber / Client **Knauf Gips KG**
Designagentur / Designagency **phocus brand contact GmbH & Co. KG**

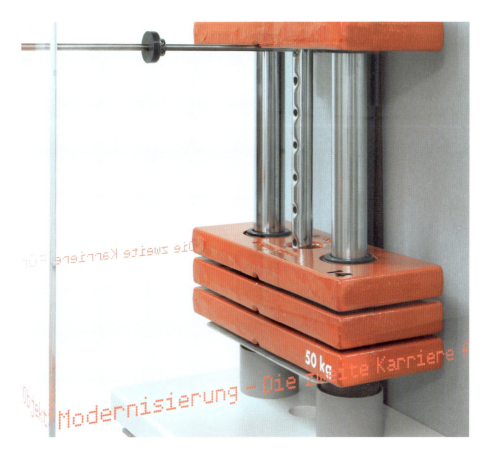

Assignment / Briefing: Concept for 6 exhibits for the travelling exhibit "Modernization on Tour." The various different exhibits are intended to impart information regarding the advantages of Knauf products in an entertaining way. To keep costs low, the exhibits must be able to be set up within 4 hours by one person. **Implementation:** Every exhibit encourages interactive critical analysis of the subject matter so that the stressed product advantages are personally perceived. The product itself becomes a museum object, thus documenting the symbiosis of functionality and aesthetics in an obvious way.

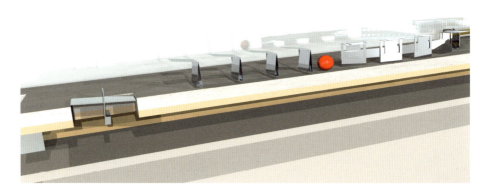

BRONZE

anika lobby furniture

Aufgabe / Briefing: Gestaltung eines modularen Wartemöbel-Programmes, das den Raumsituationen neuer Architekturen und ihren Anforderungen nach Klarheit und Reduktion auf das Wesentliche gerecht wird. **Umsetzung:** Formal reduziert auf das Wesentliche, steht ANIKA für eine architektonische Gestaltung. Markantes Element der Möbelfamilie ist ihre schlanke Geometrie.

Thema / Subject **Wartemöbel-Programm** • Auftraggeber / Client **Kokuyo Co., Ltd.**
Designagentur / Designagency **f/p design gmbh**

Assignment / Briefing: Design of a modular lobby furniture program which meets the space situations of new architectures and the requirement for clearness and reduction on the essentials.
Implementation: Reduced to the bare essentials, the ANIKA line of furniture stands for an architectonic design. The distinctive element is the slim geometry.

Adidas performance stage „nothing is impossible"

Aufgabe / Briefing: Der Showroom Performance Stage im Herz des Firmenstandortes Herzogenaurach dient der Präsentation der aktuellen Highligts der nächsten Saison für Händler, Mitarbeiter und Investoren. In der Concept Hall demonstriert Adidas das aktuelle Kommunikationskonzept „Nothing is impossible". Der Besucher soll für die neue Kommunikation begeistert werden und die key messages verstehen. **Umsetzung:** „Nothing is impossible" Die neue Kommunikationslinie wird durch die Idee der Faltung eines Spielfeldes im Raum umgesetzt. Die Umsetzung der Spielfeldmarkierung als dreidimensionale illuminierte Linien ermöglicht eine Gliederung des Raumes in unterschiedliche Themenbereiche und den Fokus auf die Produkt Highlights zu setzen. „Passion for sport. This is adidas" Dieser Brand wird umgesetzt durch eine räumliche dreidimensionale Collage aus den Protagonisten der Produktlinien (Spitzensportler), den neuesten Produkten, dem raumbildenden Gestaltungselement der illuminierten Spielfeldlinien, sowie der Atmosphäre (Ton und Film).

Thema / Subject **Showroom Concept Hall Herzogenaurach** • Auftraggeber / Client **Adidas AG**
Designagentur / Designagency **Atelier Brückner GmbH**

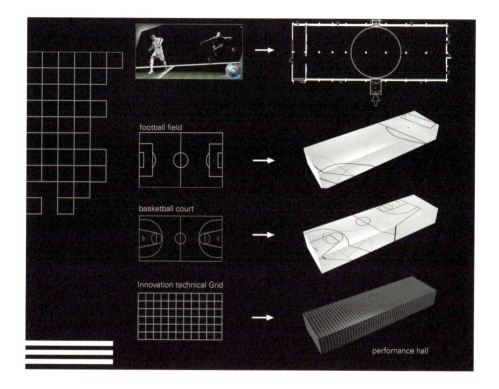

Assignment / Briefing: The showroom Performance Stage in the heart of the companies location Herzogenaurach is serving for the presentation of the upcoming seasons highlights to dealers and employees. In the Concept Hall Adidas is demonstration the actual communication concept "Nothing is impossible". The visitors ought to get excited for the new communication and ought to understand the key messages. **Implementation:** "Nothing is impossible" The new communication line is realized by folding of a life-sized playing field laid out in the given space. The three-dimensional construction of the field markings as luminous lines within the space allowed the showroom to be divided into zones for football, basketball, innovation as well as a central place for lectures and speeches, and placed the focus on the product highlights. "Passion for sport. This is adidas" The concept shows this brand by an three-dimensional collage of protagonists, the actual products and the spatial image of illuminated lines as well as a creation of atmosphere by sound and film.

Sprite.de Relaunch

Aufgabe / Briefing: Ziel des Relaunches war die authentische Verknüpfung der Marken Sprite / Sprite Zero mit dem Thema Urban Lifestyle, um Sprite / Sprite Zero auf diese Weise über das bereits gelernte Thema Basketball hinaus zu aktivieren. **Umsetzung:** Realisiert wurde diese Liaison durch den Look einer virtuellen Stadt – angelehnt an das Setting aus dem aktuellen TV-Spot - und 4 Street Künstler, die per Video persönliche Einblicke in Street Trends geben. Die Core Idea der Site „Sprite frees your mind to go your own way" wird insbesondere durch individualisierbare Wallpapers und Ecards lebendig. Beim Sprite Street Battle, das auf die Kooperation mit MTV Barrio19 einzahlt, tritt die junge Zielgruppe per Video gegeneinander an und lässt ihre persönlichen Street Skills vom Publikum bewerten.

Thema / Subject **Sprite / Sprite Zero** • Auftraggeber / Client **Coca-Cola GmbH Deutschland**
Designagentur / Designagency **argonauten G2 GmbH**

Assignment / Briefing: The aim of the relaunch was to link the Sprite/Sprite Zero brand to urban lifestyles in an authentic manner. In this way, Sprite/Sprite Zero would be associated with another topic beyond the familiar one of basketball. **Implementation:** This liaison was implemented through the look of a virtual city—based on the setting from the current TV commercial—and four street performers, who provide their personal insights into street trends via video. The main idea of the site "Sprite frees your mind to go your own way" is primarily brought to life through customized wallpapers and e-cards. In the Sprite Street Battle, that built on the cooperation with MTV Barrio19, the young target group competes against each other via video and allows the audience to rate their personal street skills..

Coke Side of life

Aufgabe / Briefing: Mit der langfristig angelegten Kampagne „Live On The Coke Side Of Life" wird „Make it real" abgelöst und die optimistische Botschaft kommuniziert, dass eine Coke „Happiness in a bottle" ist. **Umsetzung:** Mit der Markenwebsite möchte Coca-Cola eine positive Grundstimmung in Deutschland zum Dauerthema machen und inszeniert unterschwellig die Marke als Wegbereiter mit subtiler Ansprache für Teens und junge Erwachsene zwischen 14 und 24 Jahren. Das Optimismusgefühl wird durch eine adäquate Kundenansprache nach audiovisuellen, kommunikativen und inhaltlichen Aspekten erlebbar gemacht.

Thema / Subject **Coca-Cola** • Auftraggeber / Client **Coca-Cola GmbH Deutschland**
Designagentur / Designagency **argonauten G2 GmbH**

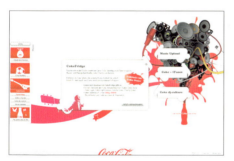

Assignment / Briefing: The long-term "Live On The Coke Side Of Life" campaign replaces "Make it real". This optimistic claim communicates the message that a Coke is "Happiness in a bottle".
Implementation: Coca-Cola wants to transform the positive mood in Germany into a recurring topic on its brand website by subliminally staging the brand as a trailblazer through subtle communication addressed to teens and young adults 14–24 years of age. The public can experience the feeling of optimism in effective customer communication shaped by audiovisual, communicative and thematic aspects.

Audi TT Lounge

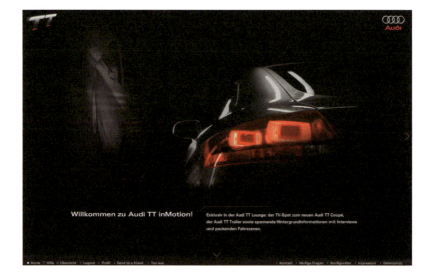

Aufgabe / Briefing: Als Teil der Launchkampagne für die zweite Generation des Audi TT war die Entwicklung einer Website gefordert, die drei unterschiedlichen Zielsetzungen gerecht werden musste: Die Website sollte zum einen weltweit qualifizierte Adressen generieren, die im Rahmen weiterer Kommunikationsmaßnahmen verwendet werden konnten. Zum zweiten sollte die Website den Usern ein intensives Produkterlebnis ermöglichen. Und drittens musste die Website so konzipiert sein, dass sie dem User während der Launchkampagne immer wieder Anreize für einen erneuten Besuch der Website geben konnte. http://www.audi.de/TT **Umsetzung:** Pur. Klar. Und auf das Wesentliche beschränkt – so lässt sich das Konzept der Audi TT Lounge zusammenfassen. Die außergewöhnliche Navigation über die Pfeiltasten der Tastatur macht störende Navigationsmenüs überflüssig, das reduzierte Design lenkt die ganze Aufmerksamkeit des Users auf das Fahrzeug und sorgt so für ein intensives Produkterlebnis. Alle Informationen zum Fahrzeug sind ohne Login für den User abzurufen, besondere Angebote wie Downloads für das Handy, Gewinnspielaktionen oder außergewöhnliche Videos erfordern eine Registrierung. Diese Zweiteilung des Angebots hat sich als erfolgreiche Mechanik für die Generierung von Userdaten erwiesen. Der registrierungspflichtige Content spielt auch als Anreiz für einen erneuten Besuch der Audi TT Lounge eine entscheidende Rolle: sein sukzessiver Ausbau bzw. Austausch, durch Newsletter kommuniziert, motiviert viele User, die Audi TT Lounge immer wieder zu besuchen.

Thema / Subject **Audi TT** • Auftraggeber / Client **Audi AG**
Designagentur / Designagency **argonauten G2 GmbH**

Assignment / Briefing: It was necessary to develop a website as part of the launch campaign for the second generation Audi TT. This website needed to meet three different aims: For one, the website was to generate qualified addresses around the world which could be used in other communication activities. Secondly, the website should enable the users to experience the product in a direct and intensive way. Finally, the website design was to motivate users to visit the website again during the launch campaign. http://www.audi.de/TT **Implementation:** Pure. Clear. And limited to the essentials – this is one way to sum up the concept of the Audi TT Lounge. Thanks to the extraordinary navigation capability using the arrow keys, irritating menus are unnecessary. The minimalist design draws the user's attention to the car, thus providing an intensive product experience. All vehicle information is available to the user without having to log in first. Special offers such as mobile phone downloads, contest participation or exceptional videos require registration. Dividing the content into two sections has proven a successful strategy for generating user data. The registration-required content also plays a decisive role in motivating users to visit the Audi TT Lounge again: A newsletter informs users of the site's gradual expansion and new content, which serves as an incentive for users to visit the site time and again.

iPray

Aufgabe / Briefing: Nie wieder Platzprobleme. Jetzt kann man die Weihnachtskrippe unterwegs mitnehmen und hat immer noch Platz für alles andere. Es ist möglich, die Figuren auf der Tischplatte zu bewegen und neue Szenen auf Basis der emotionalen Disposition der eigenen Person zu erfinden: zum Beispiel „Hinstellen" oder „Vor- und Zurückrücken". Erleben Sie Ihre Lieblingsszenen der heiligen Geschichte. Erstellen Sie unterwegs ein Theater out of the box. Starten Sie Ihr eigenes Weihnachten. Synchronisieren Sie sich mit anderen Gläubigen. Mit dem iPray sind alle Optionen sofort verfügbar.

Thema / Subject **Weihnachtsmailing** • Auftraggeber / Client **Heine/Lenz/Zizka**
Designagentur / Designagency **Heine/Lenz/Zizka**

Assignment / Briefing: Christmas on the go. Now you can take the nativity along – and still have enough space for everything else. Move around the little figures across the table. Deploy new scenes by using your personal emotional disposition: i.e. standing them up-right, pushing them back or forth. Make up your favourite nativity scenes of the holy family. Create a theater out of the box en route. Start your own personal Christmas. Sync yourself with other believers. With iPray all options are instantly on hand.

Draw me a Terrorist

Aufgabe / Briefing: Das Bewusstsein zu schärfen für die Monumentalität des Bösen und die Hoffnung auf Frieden war die Motivation des Künstlers Jeroen Teunen für das Mail Art Projekt „Draw me a Terrorist". **Umsetzung:** Das Mail Art Konzept wurde bis zur Dokumentation in aller Konsequenz umgesetzt. Das Resultat ist eine Ausstellung, die man nicht zu besuchen braucht. Die Ausstellung kommt zu den Menschen, die sich für das Projekt interessieren, direkt ins Haus und kann von dort aus in die ganze Welt weiterverschickt werden.

Thema / Subject **Ausstellungsdokumentation** • Auftraggeber / Client **Teunen Konzepte GmbH**
Designagentur / Designagency **Heine/Lenz/Zizka**

Assignment / Briefing: The artist Jeroen Teunen's motivation for creating the art project "Draw me a Terrorist" was to heighten awareness of the monumentality of evil and of the hope for peace.
Implementation: This mail art concept was implemented with consistent thoroughness from inception to documentation. The result is an exhibition which isn't to be visited in person. The exhibition visits you. It comes directly into the homes of those who are interested in the project and can then be sent on to others world wide.

BRONZE

Parabol AM

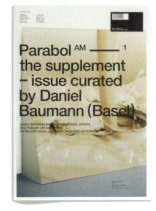

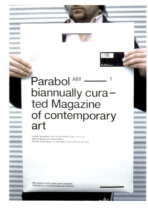

Aufgabe / Briefing: Parabol AM (Artmagazine) ist ein Magazin für internationale zeitgenössische Kunst. Ziel von Parabol AM ist es, eine Publikation zu generieren, welche in Format und Ästhetik konventionelle Magazinformate ergänzt und zeitgenössischer Kunst Raum schafft; ein Medium, das den Brückenschlag zwischen hoher inhaltlicher und gestalterischer Qualität vollzieht. Die Förderung der Auseinandersetzung mit zeitgenössischer Kunst ist Kernmotiv. Jede Ausgabe (ersch. 2x jährl.) wird von einem/r KuratorIn konzipiert. Seine Aufgabe ist es, ein zeitgenössisches Phänomen anhand künstlerischer Positionen in Bild und Wort zu thematisieren. In der Gesamtschau aller Ausgaben wird sich über die Jahre ein Spiegelbild zentraler Spotlights zeitgenössischer Kunstproduktion als zweidimensionale Ausstellung ergeben. **Umsetzung:** Mit einem Format von DIN A1 steht bei der Publikation der Bildaspekt im Vordergrund. Der Bogenoffset-Druck erinnert an die Druckqualität und das Erscheinungsbild eines Kunst-Katalogs. In diesem Punkt weicht Parabol AM sichtbar von der gewohnten Produktion eines Magazins ab. Daniel Baumann hat für die 1. Ausgabe von Parabol Künstler eingeladen, die selbst Herausgeber von Kunstzeitschriften sind. Baumann greift im ersten Heft das Thema der Vervielfältigung sowie die Auseinandersetzung mit dem scheinbar idealen Freiraum eines Künstlerheftes auf. Die Differenz zwischen dem Werk des Künstlers und seiner Publikation ist thematischer Gegenstand. Um den Editionscharakter von Parabol zu unterstreichen, sind 5 Editionen der ausgewählten Künstler beigelegt. Die Gestaltung von Parabol reduziert sich auf das Wesentliche: die zeitgenössische Kunst. Anders als herkömmliche Magazinformate steht bei Parabol die Abbildung im Vordergrund. Durch den Einsatz von Weißraum und dem Verzicht auf Farben im Layout, greift die Gestaltung nicht in die Aura der Abbildung der Arbeiten der Künstler ein. Die Wahl eines sachlichen Font, der Neuen Helvetica, unterstreicht diese Reduktion.

Thema / Subject **Internationales Kunstmagazin** • Auftraggeber / Client **section.d**
Designagentur / Designagency **section.d design. communication gmbh**

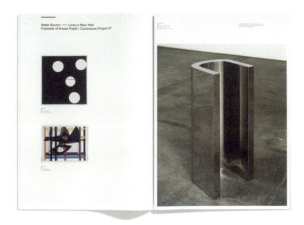

Assignment / Briefing: Parabol AM (Artmagazine) is a magazine for international contemporary art. The publication is published semi-annually in English. Each issue is devised by a curator. Each deviser's task is to examine a contemporary phenomenon in pictures and words on the basis of artistic points of view. Parabol AM centres on the representation of contemporary art in graphic space. The magazine sees itself as a network and platform. Its core motive is to promote debate about contemporary art. Over several years, the total pattern created by all the issues will result in a reflection of central spotlights of contemporary art production, like a two-dimensional exhibition.
Implementation: With its size DIN A1 (folded out), the image aspect is in the foreground of the pubication. Printing with sheet offset is reminiscent of the printing quality and general appearance of an art catalogue. In this regard, Parabol AM deviates visibly from the customary production values of a magazine. For the first issue of Parabol AM, Daniel Baumann of Basel has invited artists who work as publicists in addition to their artistic activities. In this way Baumann takes up the topic of distribution as well as the discussion about the apparently ideal free space of an art journal. The difference between the work of art and its publication is the topic of discussion. To emphasise the publishing characteristics of Parabol, five fanzines of the selected artists are attached. The design of Parabol is brought down to what matters: contemporary art. Unlike conventional magazine formats, in Parabol the image is in the foreground. With the use of white space and the absence of colours in the layout, the design does not interfere with the aura of the printed images of the artists' works. The choice of a practical font, New Helvetica, underlines this reductive approach.

MINI CONCEPT FOR THE FUTURE

Aufgabe / Briefing: Ein Grundkonzept, vier Interpretationen, vier Städte: Das Buch dokumentiert die Entwicklung von vier Studien, die für die Automobilmessen in Frankfurt, Tokio, Detroit und Genf entstanden. **Umsetzung:** Das MINI Concept ist ein Meilenstein in der Design-Geschichte von MINI. Ein – durchaus realistisches – Zukunftsauto, das Autofahren zum Erlebnis macht. Ganz im Sinne der MINI Philosophie: urban, kosmopolitisch, aufregend und funktional. Mit innovativen Materialien, einer geteilten Hecktür, multifunktionalen Cargoboxen und revolutionären Ideen für ein Fahrgefühl, das alle Sinne anspricht, setzt MINI Concept neue Maßstäbe. Auf einer Welttournee zu den wichtigsten Automobilmessen der Welt zeigte MINI Concept seine stärksten Seiten in vier verschiedenen Varianten. Die Dokumentation besticht durch eindrucksvolle Fotografien.

Auftraggeber / Client **Bayerische Motoren Werke AG, Brand Management MINI, Brand Communication** • Verlag / Publisher **HOFFMANN UND CAMPE VERLAG GmbH**

Assignment / Briefing: Documentation of four takes on a single concept – a unique concept with greater individuality. **Implementation:** First came the MINI, then the MINI Cabrio. Their go-kart exuberance and sheer sense of excitement won new friends around the world. Behind the scenes, the MINI designers were already plotting model number three. In their mind's eye was a unique concept with greater individuality and an unique concept with greater individuality and an even more ingenious use of space. The fruits of their work, the MINI Concept, embarked on a world tour to spread the message. Four takes on a single concept, picking up on the character of four locations, unveiled at four world motor shows. The designers had clearly relished the challenge, as this unique limited-edition book will testify.

Cafina ALPHA von Melitta

Aufgabe / Briefing: Gestaltung einer vollautomatischen Kaffee-Espresso-Maschine für die professionelle Gastronomie im Premiumsegment. **Umsetzung:** Visualisierung innerer funktionaler Qualitätsmerkmale durch eine kräftige, architektonische Skulptur und hochwertige Materialanmutung. Szenarische Integration in die hochwertige Gastronomie-Innenarchitektur. Harmonisierung des Bedienkonzeptes.

Thema / Subject **Vollautomatische Kaffee-Espresso-Maschine für die professionelle Gastronomie im Premiumsegment** • Auftraggeber / Client **Melitta SystemService GmbH & Co. KG** Designagentur / Designagency **Carsten Gollnick Product Design & Interior Design**

Assignment / Briefing: To design a fully automatic coffee-espresso machine for the premium segment of the food service sector. **Implementation:** Visualization of inner functional qualities by means of strong architectural features and high-quality materials. Integration into high-class interior design environment. Harmonization of the operating concept.

AUKTIONSKATALOG SAMMLUNG ENGELHARDT
DESIGN UND ALLTAGSKULTUR 50s 60s 70s

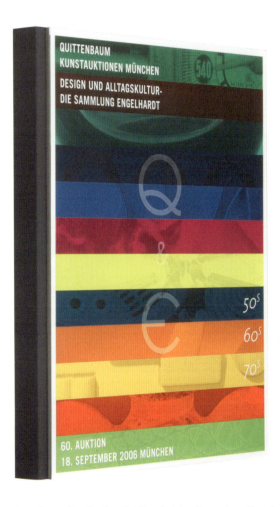

Aufgabe / Briefing: Gestaltung / Realisation Auktionskatalog Sammlung Engelhardt, Design und Alltagskultur 50s / 60s / 70s bei Quittenbaum Kunstauktionen München. **Umsetzung:** 3 Jahrzehnte Alltagskultur / Präsentation von über 600 Objekten / gegliedert in 12 Themenbereiche von Hören & Sehen über Möbel / Plastic Phantastic bis zu Mixed Cocktail auf 324 Seiten.

Thema / Subject **Auktionskatalog Sammlung Engelhardt / Auction Catalog
The Engelhardt Collection** • Auftraggeber / Client **Quittenbaum Kunstauktionen, München**
Designagentur / Designagency **Idealdesign Peter Engelhardt u. a.**
Fotografie / Photography **Peter Engelhardt, Alexander Beck**

Assignment / Briefing: Organization / realization of the auction catalog The Engelhardt Collection Design and Everyday culture 50s / 60s / 70s at Quittenbaum Art Auctions Munich. **Implementation:** 3 decades of Everyday culture / presentation of more than 600 objects / arranged in 12 topics from Listen & Watch to Furniture / Plastic Phantastic to Mixed Cocktail on 324 pages.

**Zuteilungsreif – Bausparergeschichten aus dem Südwesten /
Zuteilungsreif – Stories from the South West on building society depositors**

Aufgabe / Briefing: Katalog für eine Ausstellung im Stuttgarter Haus der Geschichte. **Umsetzung:** Die für Baden-Württemberg typische Mentalität des „Häusle-Bauens" wird auf sympathische Art dargestellt. Hinter jedem der sieben Bausparverträge steckt eine andere (Lebens-)geschichte. Diese Geschichten führen durch acht Jahrzehnte. Ein „Baukasten"-Layout wertet die notgedrungen banalen Einzelstücke dieser Erzählung optisch auf.

Thema / Subject **Ausstellungskatalog** • Auftraggeber / Client **Haus der Geschichte Baden-Württemberg** • Designagentur / Designagency **L2M3 Kommunikationsdesign GmbH**

Assignment / Briefing: Catalog for an exhibition in the Stuttgart House of History. **Implementation:** The mindset of wanting to build a house, typical for the state of Baden-Württemberg, is shown in an attractive manner. Behind each one of the seven building society contracts there is a different (life) story. These stories span eight decades. A "construction kit"-layout visually enhances the individual pieces, of this narration, which are by nature mundane.

Occhio Sento von Axelmeiselicht

axelmeiselicht

Aufgabe / Briefing: Koppeln des neuen Leuchtensystems „Occhio Sento" an die bestehende Markenstrategie des erfolgreichen Occhio Systems. **Umsetzung:** Brandrelation, Produktname, Claim, Wortmarke, Image- und Produktkataloge, Preislisten, POS Displays, Verpackungen, Messestand, Öffentlichkeitsarbeit.

Auftraggeber / Client **AML Licht + Design GmbH** • Designagentur / Designagency **Martin et Karczinski, Corporate Identity Agentur, München**

Assignment / Briefing: Couple the new "Occhio Sento" lighting system with the pre-existing brand strategy and the successful Occhio System. **Implementation:** Brand relation, product name, claim, slogan, product and application catalogues, price lists, POS displays, packaging, stand, public relations work.

Imagebroschüre für Nils Holger Moormann GmbH

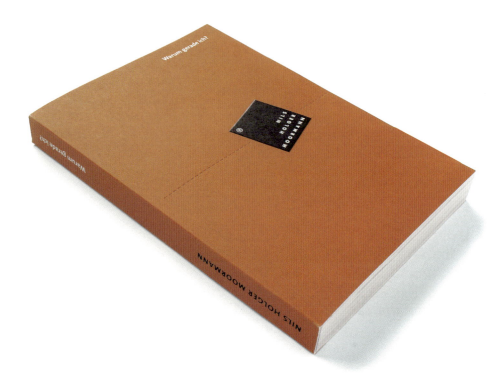

Aufgabe / Briefing: Für die im zweijährigen Turnus erscheinende Broschüre der Firma Nils Holger Moormann GmbH gibt es lediglich drei Bedingungen: – Größe DIN A 6 – das Erscheinen der Möbel, in beliebiger Art und Weise – unterschwelliger Humor. Ansonsten bleibt das Thema und die Art der Möbelpräsentation den Gestaltern frei überlassen. **Umsetzung:** Die Broschüre fragt sich, warum ausgerechnet ihr so etwas passieren mußte: Um die Besonderheiten der einzelnen Möbel herauszuarbeiten, wird jedem Möbelstück eine „Seele" – zugeordnet. Jedes Möbel erzählt ihm seine Probleme und Nöte, Sorgen und Freuden.

Thema / Subject **Imagebroschüre** • Auftraggeber / Client **Nils Holger Moormann**
Designagentur / Designagency **Jäger & Jäger**

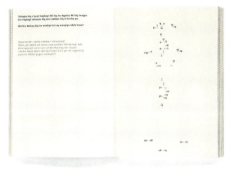

Assignment / Briefing: There are only three conditions with regard to the brochure of Nils Holger Moormann GmbH which appears every two years: – Size DIN A 6 – Appearance of the furniture in some shape or form – Humour of a subtle kind should be present. Otherwise the theme and type of furniture presentation is left to the designers. **Implementation:** The brochure is asking why it has to be like this: In order to find out their true characters, every single piece of furniture is given a „soul". And so, the catalogue has to take on the role of psychologist: Each piece of furniture confides its problems and worries, fears and joys.

INTELLIGENTE VERKNÜPFUNGEN
KOMMUNIKATION

MACHEN
WIRTSCHAFTLICHER.   Bernd Kiefer, City-Repro Medien- und Datentechnik

www.city-repro.de

BRONZE

Trick Stick

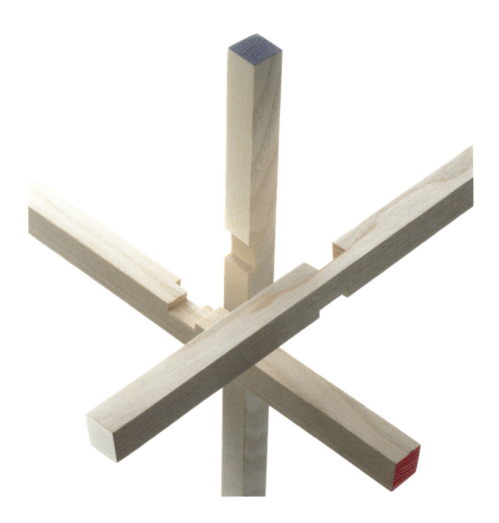

Aufgabe / Briefing: Erstellen einer Garderobe. **Umsetzung:** Trick Stick besteht aus drei Stäben, die nach traditioneller japanischer Holzverbindung ohne Werkzeug zusammengesteckt werden. So entsteht eine Ablage für Hüte, Schals und Jacken. Trick Stick steht lässig auf einem Bein, lehnt an der Wand und kann, wenn er nicht gebraucht wird, platzsparend verstaut werden

Thema / Subject **Trick Stick – Garderobe** • Auftraggeber / Client **Nils Holger Moormann**
Produktdesign / Productdesign **Markus Boge & Patrick Frey**

Assignment / Briefing: Creating a Coat Rack. **Implementation:** Trick Stick is made of three sticks, joined without tools, using a traditional japanese technique. This way, a place for hats, scarfs and jackets is created. Trick Stick stands on one leg, leans on the wall and can be put away in a space saving manner, when not needed.

Staatstheater Darmstadt in neuem Gewand

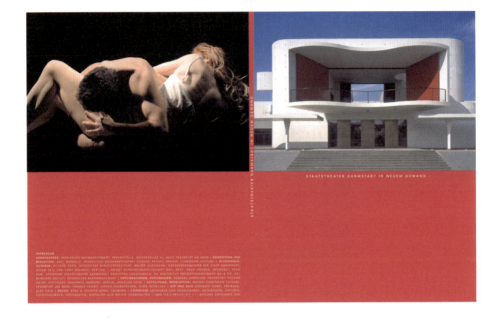

Aufgabe / Briefing: Eigentlich sollte es ein Architektur-Buch werden. Für den Umbau des Staatstheaters Darmstadt. Umbaukosten: ca. 80 Millionen Euro. Als Dokumentation und Argumentation für das Land Hessen und die Stadt Darmstadt. Aber dafür gab es kaum Geld. Und nur zwei Monate Zeit. Aber gute Fotos gab es. Als Kern-Inhalt die Spielzeit über fünf Jahre auf einer Baustelle. Und einen flexiblen, entscheidungsfreudigen Kunden. **Umsetzung:** Ein Gespräch mit allen Beteiligten: Fotografie, Architektur, Technik, Baumanagement, Theater, Land Hessen, Stadt Darmstadt. Ergebnis war kein Buch, sondern eine großzügige Broschüre mit einer etwas ungewöhnlichen Dramaturgie: Zeitstrahl für die Pflicht, erst Technik, dann Kunst und dann erst die Architektur.

Auftraggeber / Client **Hessisches Ministerium für Baumanagement**
Designagentur / Designagency **INSTANT Corporate Culture**

Assignment / Briefing: It was really supposed to be a book on architecture. On the rebuilding project at Darmstadt's State Theatre. The costs: approximately 80 million euros. To document and showcase the State of Hesse and the City of Darmstadt. But there was almost no money. And only two months to do it in. But there were some good photos. The core contents: a five-year stint on the building site. And a flexible, decisive client. **Implementation:** TA dialogue with all the parties involved: photographers, architects, engineers, site managers, the theatre people, the State of Hessen, the City of Darmstadt. The result was not a book, but a generously dimensioned brochure with a somewhat unusual dramaturgical timeline, first engineering, then art, and only then the architecture.

BRONZE

Der Sony Messeauftritt auf der IFA 2005

Aufgabe / Briefing: Messe-Neuauftritt von SONY Deutschland auf der IFA 2005. Interpretation und Inszenierung des Marken-Claims: like.no.other. Der Auftritt sollte sich vom Wettbewerb klar abgrenzen und die Kernthemen „Imaging", „Gaming", „Mobile", „Video" durch eine zielgruppengerechte Kundenansprache transportieren. Einmalige Hallenbespielung mit einem Messestand der selbsterklärend ist und ohne Stand- und Promotionspersonal funktionieren soll. **Umsetzung:** Die Besucher erleben in Halle 18 auf 3.800 qm allein die Marke SONY, in dem sie zwischen die Stoffbahnen eines sich bewegenden Raumes gehen und Erlebnisräume / Erlebniswelten entdecken. Die Botschaften der Marke korrespondieren spielerisch mit den Wünschen und Sehnsüchten der Verbraucher und Standbesucher: Musik, Filme, individuelle Lebensgefühle. Innerhalb der Interaktion (Erlebnis) entwickelt sich eine Identität zwischen Besucher und SONY.

Thema / Subject **Messeauftritt** • Auftraggeber / Client **Sony Deutschland GmbH**
Designagentur / Designagency **Design Company Agentur GmbH, München**

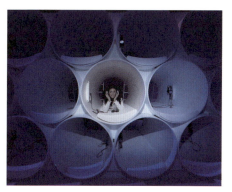

Assignment / Briefing: SONY Germany's new exhibit at the IFA 2005 trade show. Interpretation and staging of the brand claim: like.no.other. The exhibit was designed to set SONY apart from the competition and convey the core themes of "Imaging", "Gaming", "Mobile" and "Video" by addressing specific target groups. A unique performance in a booth that is self-explanatory and does not need to be manned by trade show personnel or promoters. **Implementation:** In Hall 18, visitors experience only the SONY brand in a space measuring 3,800 square meters, where they enter a moving space and discover remarkable new worlds. The brand's messages playfully express the wishes and dreams of consumers and visitors to the booth through music, film and individual attitudes toward life. The interaction (experience) helps forge a bond between the visitors and SONY.

DAS GUTE STÜCK

AWARD

AVIANA, Serie 5976

Aufgabe / Briefing: Produkte, die in Flugzeugen eingesetzt werden unterliegen besonders strengen Anforderungen. Dies gilt auch für so vermeintlich einfache Produkte wie Rollen für Servicetrolleys. Gewichtsersparnis, Zuverlässigkeit und ein reibungsloser Servicebetrieb an Bord waren die zu erfüllenden Kriterien. **Umsetzung:** Besondere Merkmale wurden realisiert: extreme Gewichtsersparnis gegenüber der herkömmlichen Stahlrolle – deutlich höhere Festigkeitswerte innerhalb der geforderten Normen durch die seitlichen Radführungen – kein Verkeilen beim Herausziehen aus den Galleycompartments – deutliche besseres Reinigungsverhalten durch die geschlossene und glatte Gehäuseform – Anpassung der Farbgebung an das Corporate Design – dauerhafter Schutz vor Korrosion durch rostfreie Werkstoffe – zertifiziert nach FAR/JAR 25853 für Flammbeständigkeit.

Thema / Subject **Inflight Trolley Rolle „AVIANA"** • Auftraggeber / Client **TENTE-ROLLEN GmbH**
Produktdesign / Productdesign **Squareone GmbH**

Assignment / Briefing: Extremely high demands are placed on products, materials and processes which are concerned with aeroplanes and air traffic. This also applies to castors for inflight trolleys. Reduced weight and increased reliability have top priority for airlines here. Furthermore, there are additional criteria which are crucial for smooth service on board. **Implementation:** The new synthetic trolley castor "AVIANA" offers the following benefits: extreme weight saving in comparison to conventional steel castors – higher mechanical stability within the demanded norms – no seizing of the castors when pulling out of the galleycompartments – due to the lateral wheel leads – better cleaning behaviour because of the closed and smooth shaped housing – colour can be matched to corporate design – maintenance-free due to use of corrosion-free components – certified according to FAR/JAR for flammability.

AWARD

"216plus / 217plus"

Aufgabe / Briefing: Sal. Oppenheim ist eine der führenden Privatbanken Europas. Ziel war es, ein hochwertiges, aufmerksamkeitsstarkes und unterhaltendes Magazin zu schaffen, welches dem anspruchsvollen Selbstverständnis des Hauses Sal. Oppenheim entspricht. **Umsetzung:** Der Gestaltungsauftritt des Kundenmagazins kommuniziert mit seinem klassischen, repräsentativen Charakter in unaufdringlicher Weise die im Hause Sal. Oppenheim bewusst gelebten Werte Tradition, Innovation und Exklusivität.

Thema / Subject **Kundenmagazin der Privatbank Sal. Oppenheim jr. & Cie**
Auftraggeber / Client **Sal. Oppenheim jr. & Cie. KGaA**
Designagentur / Designagency **Simon & Goetz Design GmbH & Co. KG**

Assignment / Briefing: Sal. Oppenheim is one of the leading private banks in Europe. Task was to create a premium, attention-grabbing and entertaining magazine, which communicates the sophisticated self-conception of Sal. Oppenheim. **Implementation:** With its classic, representative character the magazine's design communicates the consciously lived values tradition, innovation and exclusivness in an unintrusive way.

Mr. Proper „Zebrastreifen"

Aufgabe / Briefing: Ausgangssituation: Reinigungsmittel gehören zum Low Interest Segment, deshalb muss um die Aufmerksamkeit und das Interesse der Konsumenten gekämpft werden. Die Verbraucher sind außerdem gelangweilt von der gewöhnlichen Haushaltsreiniger Werbung. Deshalb musste ein aufmerksamkeitsstarkes und außergewöhnliches Medium für die Kommunikationsmaßnahme ausgewählt werden. Ziel war es, Meister Proper Haushaltsreiniger auf eine plakative Art und Weise als kraftvollen Reiniger zu positionieren. **Umsetzung:** Um den Konsumenten auf einer ungewöhnlichen Art und Weise zu begegnen, wurde das sogenannte Medium „Ambient Media" ausgewählt. Es wurde ein Streifen eines Zebrastreifens strahlend weiß eingefärbt und mit dem Meister Proper Logo versehen. Beim Betreten des Zebrastreifens soll der Konsument auf eine überraschende Art von der Reinigungskraft von Meister Proper Haushaltsreiniger überzeugt werden.

Auftraggeber / Client **Procter & Gamble**

Assignment / Briefing: Situation: Cleaning products belong to the low investment category, and therefore there is a struggle for the customer's attention. The consumers are also bored by the usual cleaning-product advertisement. Therefore a unique media has to be chosen for the communication that has to guarantee a high awareness. The aim was to position Meister Proper as a strong cleaner in the Market, by demonstrating its power and effectiveness in a striking way. **Implementation:** To reach the consumer in an unusual way, the so called Medium "ambient media" had been chosen. A zebra crossing was painted shining white, and marked with the Meister Proper icon. With trespassing the zebra crossing, the consumer will be convinced of the cleaning powers of Meister Proper in a surprising way.

DIE EMPFEHLUNG EINES FREUNDES

GNORIERE DEINEN GESCHMACK.

Bernhard Mittelmann, alfi GmbH

www.alfi.de

AWARD

Real Toys „Feuerwehrwagen", „Bagger", „Müllwagen"

Aufgabe / Briefing: Kinder und Erwachsene davon überzeugen, dass die Spielzeug-Fahrzeuge bei Toys 'R' Us so aussehen wie die echten Großen. **Umsetzung:** Um Spielzeug so echt wie möglich aussehen zu lassen, gibt es eigentlich nur eine Möglichkeit: Zeig es so als sei es real. Dafür nutzten wir reale Fahrzeuge, befestigten überdimensionale Preisschilder daran und ließen sie durch die City fahren.

Thema / Subject **Imagewerbung** • Auftraggeber / Client **Toys 'R' Us**

Assignment / Briefing: Show kids and parents how real the toy car range at Toys 'R' Us looks.
Implementation: When it comes to real toys, there's just one option to make it look real: be real. We used real cars, attached price tags to them and let them drive through the city.

Stier

Aufgabe / Briefing: Aufgabe war es eine Anzeige für die Mallorca-Zeitung zu entwickeln, die auf ungewöhnliche Weise kommunizieren sollte, dass es bereits drei Orion-Stores in Spanien gibt.
Umsetzung: Herausgekommen ist eine Anzeige, die einen prächtigen Stier zeigt, das spanische Symbol schlechthin, der statt eines üblichen Nasenrings einen, äääh, Cockri ..., ääh, etwas zeigt was es eben nur bei Orion zu kaufen gibt.

DAS GUTE STÜCK

Auftraggeber / Client **Orion Versand GmbH & Co.KG**
Designagentur / Designagency **Heye & Partner GmbH**

Assignment / Briefing: The assignment was to create an advert for the Mallorca newspaper, in which it was communicated in an unusual fashion, that there are 3 Orion stores in Spain.
Implementation: What came out was a magnificent bull, the symbol of Spain par excellence, but instead of the typical nose ring, it had a certain type of "intimate" ring Naturally, available at Orion.

Das Ende des Schweigens – Der Frankfurter Auschwitz-Prozess 1963-65

Aufgabe / Briefing: Im Frankfurter Auschwitz-Prozess von 1963 bis 1965 erfuhr die Weltöffentlichkeit erstmals Einzelheiten der Massenmorde und Verbrechen im Vernichtungslager Auschwitz. Das multimediale Webspecial „Das Ende des Schweigens" dokumentiert die Äußerungen von Überlebenden des Holocaust und die Versuche der Angeklagten, sich zu verteidigen. **Umsetzung:** 67 interaktive Text-Ton-Bild-Collagen lassen scheinbar Unfassbares erlebbar werden. In einer Website, die durch die ungeschminkte Konfrontation mit dem Material ein intensives emotionales Erlebnis entstehen lässt.

Thema / Subject **Der Frankfurter Auschwitz-Prozess 1963-65** • Auftraggeber / Client
Hessischer Rundfunk • Designagentur / Designagency **BlueMars – Gesellschaft für digitale Kommunikation mbH**

Assignment / Briefing: It was not until the Frankfurt Auschwitz trials, which took place from 1963 to 1965, that the world first learned all the details involving the mass murders and crimes committed at the Auschwitz extermination camp. "The End of Silence" is a multimedia web special that documents statements made by Holocaust survivors and the attempts by the accused to defend themselves. **Implementation:** Sixty-seven interactive collages of texts, sounds and images allow the seemingly incomprehensible to be experienced in a website whose unvarnished confrontation with the material produces an intense and emotional experience.

LAMY dialog 2 Tintenroller / LAMY dialog 2 Rollerball pen

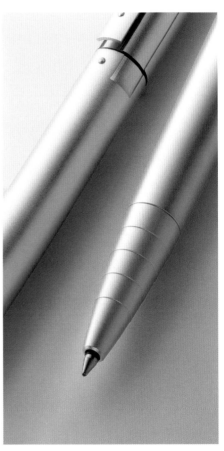

Aufgabe / Briefing: Entwicklung eines kappenlosen Tintenrollers mit Drehmechanik in einem Metallgehäuse. Funktionsprinzip: Mine raus / Clip rein bzw. Mine rein / Clip raus mit jeweils einer Drehbewegung ohne Umgreifen. **Umsetzung:** Mittels einer aufwendigen Mechanik im Inneren wurde in Kombination mit der klaren Formsprache ein in seinen Funktionen eindeutiges und seiner Materialwahl unverwechselbares Schreibgerät geschaffen.

Thema / Subject **Tintenroller / Rollerball pen** • Auftraggeber / Client **C. Josef LAMY GmbH, Heidelberg** • Produktdesign / Productdesign **Knud Holscher, Dänemark**

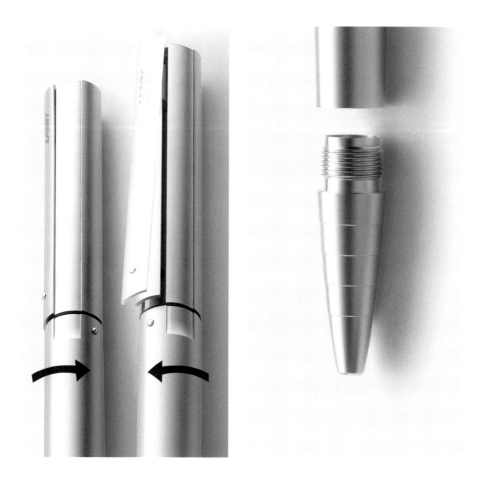

Assignment / Briefing: Development of a full-metal rollerball pen with a retractable clip. In the writing position, the rollerball is extended and the clip retracted. When the rollerball is retracted, the clip is raised. **Implementation:** By combining an intelligent inner mechanism with a clear outlined body and a high-quality material the rollerball pen is a distinctive easy to use writing instrument with clear features.

T-World – Virtuelles Haus der T-Com

Aufgabe / Briefing: Produkte und Dienstleistungen der T-Com sollten in ausgewählten T-Punkten durch eine erlebnisorientierte Präsentation interaktiv dargestellt werden. **Umsetzung:** Ein virtuelles Wohnhaus wurde geschaffen, durch das sich der Nutzer per Touch bewegen kann. Unterschiedliche Räume dienen zur Navigation. Über Animationen werden Anwendungen der Produkte im Umfeld alltäglicher Nutzenszenarien erklärt.

Auftraggeber / Client **Deutsche Telekom AG**
Designagentur / Designagency **people interactive GmbH**

Assignment / Briefing: With an experience orientated and interactive presentation products and services of the T-Com are to be presented in selected T-Punkts. **Implementation:** A virtual house was created, through which the user can move around by touching the screen. Different rooms serve as the navigation. Animations explain the use of the products in an everyday life environment.

T-Gallery Intranetpräsenz

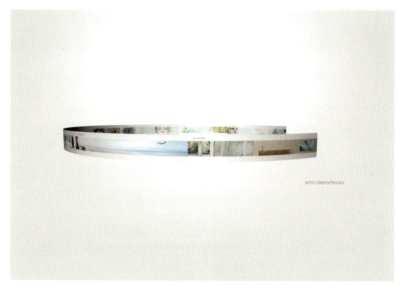

Aufgabe / Briefing: Die T-Gallery ist ein Innovationsforum der Deutschen Telekom in der Bonner Zentrale. Die gleichnamige Intranetpräsenz soll Einblicke in die Ausstellung geben und die Themen und Exponate den Mitarbeitern interaktiv nahe bringen. **Umsetzung:** In Anlehnung an den Grundriss der Ausstellung bestimmt ein animiertes Image-Band Gestaltung und Navigation der Site. Exponate lassen sich interaktiv bedienen und geben, ergänzt durch Animationen, Einblicke in Lebenswelten von Morgen.

Auftraggeber / Client **Deutsche Telekom AG**
Designagentur / Designagency **people interactive GmbH**

Assignment / Briefing: The Deutsche Telekom presents product innovations in the T-Gallery, a forum and exhibition in Bonn. The respective intranet is to give insights on the exhibition and make the themes and exhibits accessible to the employees in an interactive manner. **Implementation:** An animated image band takes up the layout of the exhibition and defines design and navigation of the site. Animations and exhibits which can be used interactively give the user insights on tomorrow's everyday life.

Messestand steute Medica 2005

Aufgabe / Briefing: Entwurf und Realisation eines Messestandes für den Geschäftsbereich Medizintechnik der steute Schaltgeräte GmbH & Co. KG.

Thema / Subject **Messestand** • Auftraggeber / Client **Steute Schaltgeräte GmbH & Co.KG**
Designagentur / Designagency **Büro Longjaloux GmbH**

Assignment / Briefing: Outline and Realisation of the exhibition stand in the medical Equipment Unit of steute Schaltgeräte GmbH & Co. KG.

Bravo Charlie – Bar / Club

Aufgabe / Briefing: Gestalten Sie ein Corporate Design für eine Bar und einen Club im ehemaligen Lufthansa-Terminal in Stuttgart. Das Design sollte einzigartig aber nicht aufgesetzt sein. Es sollte emotional aufladen und ein guter Freund werden können… **Umsetzung:** Die Anfangsbuchstaben von „Bar" und „Club" buchstabiert man im Pilotenalphabet „Bravo" und „Charlie". Ein Name wie ein Ausruf! Ein Logo wie eine Sprechblase. Ein persönlicher Name. Ein raumgreifendes Corporate Design – vielfältig inspiriert von der Welt des Fliegens und der Flugzeuge – das immer für direkte Kommunikation sorgt. Ob auf Streichhölzern, Speisekarten, Tabletts und Geschirr, als Interior auf allen Wänden und Decken – oder auch gerne als Sticker im öffentlichen Raum.

Thema / Subject **Bar / Club** • Auftraggeber / Client **Bravo Charlie Betriebsgesellschaft mbH**
Designagentur / Designagency **i_d buero**

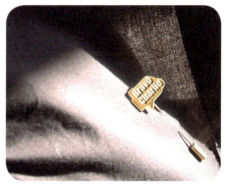

Assignment / Briefing: We where asked to do the Corporate Design for a Bar and Club in the former Lufthansa-Terminal in Stuttgart. The Look was meant to be unique but not artificial. It should be emotional and be able to become a good friend to the guests. **Implementation:** Spelled in the pilots alphabet the initials of the two words "Bar" and "Club" are BRAVO and CHARLIE. A name like an interjection! A logo like a speech bubble! A logo that always arranges for direct communication. An all-embracing Corporate Design – inspired by the aviation world. Printed on glasses, business cards, menues, T-shirts or reinterpreted as street art.

TT unseen

Aufgabe / Briefing: Entwicklung eines Kommunikationsmittels, das die mediale Inszenierung des TT auf dem design annual 2006 kommunikativ unterstützt. **Umsetzung:** 10 Künstler entwickeln ihre Vision eines urbanen Ortes. Die fiktiven Orte werden medial zur Inszenierung des TT Showrooms eingesetzt und mit einem hochwertigen Miniatur Katalog dokumentiert.

Thema / Subject **Audi TT** • Auftraggeber / Client **Audi AG**
Designagentur / Designagency **Mutabor Design GmbH**

Assignment / Briefing: To develop a means of communication that gives communicative support to the media-based presentation of the TT at the 2006 design annual. **Implementation:** 10 artists develop their visions of an urban location. The fictitious locations are used in the media to present the TT showrooms and documented with a high-quality miniature catalogue.

AWARD

GOLF LOVES EUROPE
EUROPE LOVES GOLF

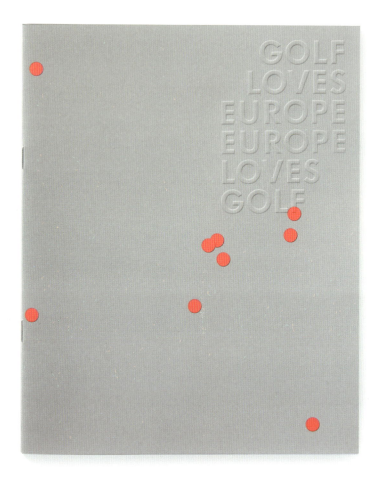

Aufgabe / Briefing: Redaktionelles Mittel zur Emotionalisierung des VW Golf. **Umsetzung:** Internationale Fotoschulen wurden eingeladen, um den Golf in einem landestypischen Sujet darzustellen. Die Ergebnisse aus ganz Europa zeigen politische wie gesellschaftliche Interpretationen.

Thema / Subject **Europäischer Fotowettbewerb** • Auftraggeber / Client **Volkswagen AG**
Designagentur / Designagency **Mutabor Design GmbH**

Assignment / Briefing: Editorial means of emotionalising the VW Golf. **Implementation:** International photographic schools were invited to present the Golf in situations typical of their respective countries. The results from all over Europe demonstrate political and social interpretations.

filigraner Holzstuhl act

Aufgabe / Briefing: Aufgabe war, einen filigranen, stapelbaren und sehr eleganten Holzstuhl zu entwerfen, der die Grenzen des Machbaren im Holzbereich auslotet, dabei trotzdem äußerst stabil ist und sich für den rauen Einsatz im Objektbereich eignet. **Umsetzung:** Für die Umsetzung wurde Schichtholz gewählt, da die Verleimung äußerst geringe Querschnitte bei hoher Stabilität erlaubt. Querschnitte wurden dort vergrößert, wo große Kräfte auftreten und dort verjüngt, wo sich Kräfte minimieren. Neu und ungewöhnlich für Schichtholztechnik sind zudem die nach allen Seiten sich verjüngenden Verläufe. Wegen der geringen Materialstärken wurden die Verbindungen von Sitz und Rücken und die Armteilanbindungen mittels völlig neuer innovativer, nicht sichtbarer Verbindungstechnik gelöst. Dank dieser Techniken gelingt eine formal filigrane Aussage die den Stuhl sehr eigenständig wirken lässt.

Auftraggeber / Client **Brunner GmbH** • Produktdesign / Productdesign **Wolfgang C.R. Mezger**

Assignment / Briefing: The challenge was, to design a filigree, stackable and highly elegant wooden chair which defines new boundaries of technical feasibility, being robust and able to resist a rude use in contract furniture applications. **Implementation:** The choice was given to a plywood construction due to the reason that this solution provides highest levels of stability and marginal material thicknesses at the same time. Cross sections of the seat shell have been expanded where strong force effects apply, other sections have been minimized for enhanced elegance. The all-side tapered gradient is a technical revolution and exceptional technical novelty for plywood constructions. The minimized material thicknesses necessitate a new innovative and invisible technique for joining the seat, backrest and armrest elements. Thanks to this technique the chair provides an independant and peerless architectural appeal.

3xICH – Ben Oyne & Students

Ben Oyne & Students. Highlights einer Workshoptournee über inszenierte Fotografie.

Aufgabe / Briefing: Inszenieren Sie drei Bilder, wobei Sie selbst nicht nur Fotograf, sondern auch Darsteller, Szenarist, Kostüm- und Maskenbildner sind. Obwohl es sich immer um die gleiche Person handelt, sollen die drei Fotos den Eindruckvermitteln, als sähen wir drei verschiedene Menschen, äußerlich dargestellt durch unterschiedliche soziale Veränderungen und durch Wechsel von Milieu, Dekor und Kleidung. Die charakterliche Transformation könnte durch Mimik und Körperhaltung unterstützt werden, aber vor allem durch eine glaubwürdige Projektion von innerseelischer Veränderung. Basis der Aufgabenstellung bildeten die fotografischen Transformationen von Cindy Sherman. Mit geringsten Mitteln, ohne aufwändige Arrangements und ohne Dekorationen sollten die Studenten ans Ziel kommen. **Umsetzung:** Zwischen 2003 und 2005 besuchte der schwedische Fotograf und Filmemacher Ben Oyne mit seinem Workshopprojekt elf deutsche Lehranstalten für Fotografie, Design und Kommunikation. 312 Studenten beteiligten sich an der Inszenierungsaufgabe „3xICH" und reichten 936 Arbeiten ein. 64 Studenten zeigen in diesem Buch eine Auslese von 192 Fotos.

Thema / Subject **Buch** • Auftraggeber / Client **Fachhochschule Wiesbaden, Fachbereich Design Informatik Medien**

Assignment / Briefing: Produce three photgraphs in which you are not merely active as the photographer but as the performer, scenarist, costume designer and make-up artist. Although all are one and the same person, the three photographs should impart the impression as though we are viewing three different persons outwardly represented through various social changes and through variations in the setting, surroundings and attire. The transformations in character may be augmented by gestures and posture but, above all, should be supported through a credible projection of inner metamorphosis. The photographic transformations by Cindy Sherman formed the basis of the task definition. The students should attempt to achieve the desired objective with only the most basic of resources and without extensive arrangements or decorations. **Implementation:** From 2003-2005 the Swedish photographer and filmmaker Ben Oyne visited eleven German universities where photography, design and communication are taught and presented his workshop project. 312 students participated in the staging exercise "3xICH" ("3xME") and submitted 936 results. 64 students present a selection of 192 photographs in this book.

Motiv-ator

Aufgabe / Briefing: Eine kleine Agentur will zeigen, dass sie Großes kann. Dass dies mit einem einfachen Mailing nicht erreicht wird, war schnell klar. Es galt also neben der Agenturdarstellung auch den T-Shirt Shop vorzustellen, und: die Lektüre soll einen zusätzlichen, persönlichen Nutzen haben.
Umsetzung: „Motiv-ator" ist etwas Besonderes. Es ist eine Agenturdarstellung, die ein Magazin ist, das ein Katalog ist. „Motiv-ator" schafft es, das Leistungsvermögen der Agentur zu demonstrieren, ohne darüber zu reden. So wird aus einem Sales Tool ein spannendes und schönes Magazin.

Thema / Subject **Motiv-ator** • Auftraggeber / Client **New Cat Orange**
Designagentur / Designagency **New Cat Orange**

Assignment / Briefing: A small agency wants to show that it can handle something big. Which of course can not be achieved with a simple direct mail. So on top of presenting the agency, its t-shirt shop had to be introduced, as well. And on top, reading it was to deliver an additional, personal benefit. **Implementation:** "Motiv-ator" is something special. It's an agency presentation that is a magazine that is a catalogue. "Motiv-ator" is able to show what the agency is capable of – without even talking about it. Consequently, a simple sales tool is turned into an inspiring and beautiful magazine.

Uniplan VIP Lounge

Aufgabe / Briefing: In den Räumen der Agentur sind zahlreiche Werke der agentureigenen Kunstsammlung „Uniplan Art Collection" ausgestellt. Aufgrund dieser engen Verbindung zur Kunst, entschied sich Uniplan, Sponsor der ART COLOGNE zu werden, um in eine exklusive VIP-Lounge zu laden. **Umsetzung:** Für jedes der präsentierten Werke wurde ein eigener Raum, eine Art Kubus konzipiert. Diese individuell konfektionierten Räume ergaben in der Addition ein Raumgefüge, dessen Zwischenräume als kommunikative Anlaufstelle für Agentur und Kunden dienten.

Thema / Subject **Raumkonzeption** • Auftraggeber / Client **Uniplan International GmbH & Co. KG** • Architektur / Architecture **Ole Schilling**

Assignment / Briefing: A number of pieces from the company's own "Uniplan art collection" are displayed in rooms throughout the agency. This close connection to art prompted Uniplan to be a sponsor of ART COLOGNE and to invite guests to the exclusive VIP lounge. **Implementation:** A number of pieces from the company's own "Uniplan art collection" are displayed in rooms throughout the agency. This close connection to art prompted Uniplan to be a sponsor of ART COLOGNE and to invite guests to the exclusive VIP lounge.

Montblanc Relaunch

Aufgabe / Briefing: Der neue Internet-Auftritt von Montblanc ist an die Markenpositionierung und das aktuelle Erscheinungsbild von Montblanc angepasst. Er beweist, dass das Montblanc-Signet längst nicht mehr nur für edle Schreibgeräte steht, sondern für eine in viele Luxusgüter-Bereiche diversifizierte Marke. **Umsetzung:** Das sich durch die gesamte Anwendung durchtragende Teaser-Konzept ermöglicht bereits auf der Homepage die Abbildung des gesamten Spektrums unterschiedlicher Themen. Das Herz des Auftritts bildet der Produktkatalog mit über 1.400 Artikeln in sieben verschiedenen Produktkategorien, der durch eine eigens entwickelte Datenbank gespeist wird. Hier kann man sich jeden einzelnen Artikel anschauen und anhand einer Toolbox Infos und Artikelvarianten aufrufen sowie Zusatzfunktionen wie Zoomen oder 3D-Ansichten nutzen.

Thema / Subject **Montblanc Relaunch** • Auftraggeber / Client **Montblanc International GmbH**
Designagentur / Designagency **Elephant Seven AG**

Assignment / Briefing: Montblanc's new website is designed to reflect the new brand positioning and Montblanc's current image. It proves that for some time now, the Montblanc logo has not only stood for fine writing instruments; it represents a brand which has diversified into a range of luxury goods. **Implementation:** The teaser concept runs through the whole application and allows the whole spectrum of different topics to be incorporated into the homepage. The heart of the website is the extensive product catalogue with more than 1,400 articles in seven different product categories which draws on a specially developed database. This allows interested customers to look at any Montblanc item and call up information and different product versions using a toolbox. They can also use extra tools such as zooming in or 3-D views.

Mercedes-Benz CL-Klasse Special

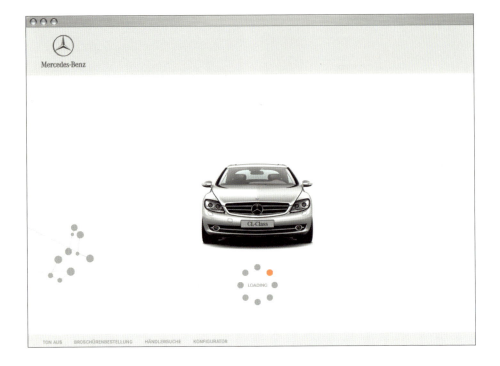

Aufgabe / Briefing: „Wer davon träumt, das Beste noch zu steigern, muss in mehr als eine Richtung denken." Eindrucksvolles Ergebnis dieser Denkweise: die neue CL-Klasse von Mercedes-Benz.
Umsetzung: Ein solches Ausnahmefahrzeug braucht natürlich eine einzigartige Online-Präsentation. Eine, die den langen Entstehungsprozess und das beeindruckende Resultat auf emotionale und fesselnde Art rüberbringt. So kann der Anwender in einer flexiblen Mind mapping Navigation den weiten Weg vom Traum zur Wirklichkeit nachvollziehen - und sich in rasanten Kamerafahrten um eines der faszinierendsten Autos unserer Zeit von dessen optischer und technischer Überlegenheit einfangen lassen.

Thema / Subject **CL-Klasse Special** • Auftraggeber / Client **DaimlerChrysler Vertriebsorganisation Deutschland** • Designagentur / Designagency **Elephant Seven AG**

Assignment / Briefing: "Anyone who dreams of pushing the limits has to think outside the box." The new CL-Class by Mercedes-Benz is the result of exactly this sort of thinking. **Implementation:** Such an extraordinary vehicle requires an online introduction as unique as itself – one that illustrates the long development process and the impressive finished product in an emotional and gripping way. Flexible mind-map navigation demonstrates the long journey from dream to reality, while the aesthetic and technical superiority of one of the most fascinating cars of our time captivates viewers using impressive camera shots.

smart Gebrauchtwagen, Banner „Will los"

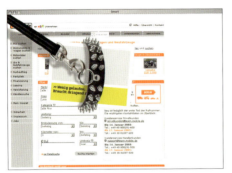

Aufgabe / Briefing: Der response-orientierte Banner zeigt einen von vielen Vorteilen auf, mit der ein smart – auch als Gebrauchtwagen – aufwarten kann. **Umsetzung:** Über das Jahr hinweg werden einzelne Vorteile einfach und spannend herausgearbeitet. Die Banner wurden auf Automobilseiten und Gebrauchtwagenbörsen geschaltet, um Interessenten ab 25 Jahren und junge Familien zu begeistern und auf die Onlinesuche zu leiten. Der außerordentliche Erfolg im Sinne von Response und Conversionrate bestätigt den Einzelansatz mit starkem Formatbezug.

Auftraggeber / Client **DaimlerChrysler Vertriebsorganisation Deutschland**
Designagentur / Designagency **Elephant Seven AG**

Assignment / Briefing: The response-oriented banner demonstrates one of the wide range of advantages which a smart offers – even as a second-hand car. **Implementation:** Over the year, the individual advantages of the smart are brought out in a simple yet exciting way. The banners were placed on auto sites and used car listings in order to get over-25s and young families interested and to prompt them to take a further look online. The extraordinary success as far as the response and the conversion rate are concerned confirms our attempt to strongly bring out individual characteristics in the banner format.

o2 Germany Messeauftritt CeBIT 2006

Aufgabe / Briefing: Die visuelle Präsenz von o2 Germany auf der CeBIT 2006 sollte durch die konzeptionelle Weiterentwicklung des Messeauftritts gegenüber dem Vorjahr noch verstärkt werden.
Umsetzung: Die Deckenkonstruktion bildete den Blickfang des Standes: ein über 1.000 m² großer Farbbildschirm aus rund 28.000 Pixel, über den Videobilder und Textsequenzen liefen. Mit Spiegelglas beschichtete Theken verstärkten seine optische Präsenz.

Thema / Subject **Messeauftritt** • Auftraggeber / Client **o2 (Germany) GmbH & Co. OHG**
Designbüro / Design studio **KMS** • Architektur / Architecture **Schmidhuber + Partner**

Assignment / Briefing: The visual presence of o2 Germany at CeBIT 2006 should have been enhanced by a further development of the concept of the previous year's exhibit. **Implementation:** The eye catcher of the exhibition stand was the ceiling structure, a 1,000 m² color display composed of about 28,000 pixels, showing video images and textual sequences. Counters covered with mirror glass enhanced its visual presence.

Zeig' uns etwas Neues

Aufgabe / Briefing: Die Aufgabenstellung entwickelte sich aus der Frage, wie auf dem großen Markt der Kommunikationsdesigner diejenigen zu gewinnen sind, die am besten zu unserem Büro passen.
Umsetzung: Wir lassen in der entsprechenden Rubrik auf unserer Website einen kurzen Film laufen, der repräsentiert, was wir sind: ein kreatives Büro, das seine Mitarbeiter fördert und von ihnen Selbstständigkeit und Eigeninitiative erwartet – durch nichts anderes ist dieser Film entstanden.

Thema / Subject **Kurzfilm** • Auftraggeber / Client **KMS** • Designagentur / Designagency **KMS**

Assignment / Briefing: The objective arose from the question of how to find those candidates from the large market of communications designers who best match the requirements of our design studio. **Implementation:** We show a brief film in the relevant section of our website. It represents what we are: a creative studio, which promotes its employees and expects independent thinking and initiative. This is just how this film came about.

ENTRY 2006

Aufgabe / Briefing: Im Sommer 2006 fand in Essen das erste Weltforum für Design und Architektur statt: ENTRY2006. **Umsetzung:** Für ENTRY haben wir das Erscheinungsbild einschließlich des Namens entworfen. Ausgangspunkt ist das Bildzeichen: ein rotes Y (der Endbuchstabe von ENTRY), das dreidimensional als Koordinatenkreuz realisiert wird. Es verbindet so die Bereiche des (Typo-) Graphischen und des Räumlichen, den jeweiligen Ur-Domänen von Design und Architektur.

Thema / Subject **Erscheinungsbild** • Auftraggeber / Client **Ausstellungsgesellschaft Zollverein mbH**
Designagentur / Designagency **KMS**

Assignment / Briefing: In summer 2006, Essen hosted the first World Exposition for Design and Architecture: ENTRY2006. **Implementation:** For ENTRY, we created the name and the corporate design. The starting point of our conception is the distinctive symbol of a red Y (the final letter in ENTRY), which, rendered in three dimensions, appears as a system of coordinates. It thus connects the ideas of the graphic (plane) with that of the spatial, the respective original domains of design and architecture.

WIR STELLEN MIT DESIGN SYSTEM
VERBINDUNGEN HER – SONS

ATISCH(E)
EIGENTLICH NICHTS.

Jürgen Blümel, artefakt Offenbach

www.artefakt-offenbach.de

3-STRIPES ARE COMING!

Aufgabe / Briefing: Wir wurden von dem Sportartikelhersteller adidas beauftragt, die internationale Eröffnungskampagne für die adidas Performance Centres zu erarbeiten. **Umsetzung:** Wir haben das Konzept „3 STRIPES ARE COMING!" entwickelt, das die jeweils neue adidas-Präsenz als Herannahen der drei Streifen visualisiert. Auf den Plakaten sind Szenen aus der jeweiligen Stadt zu sehen, in denen überdimensionale adidas-Streifen über Gebäude und Straßen verlaufen.

Thema / Subject **Shop-Eröffnungskampagne** • Auftraggeber / Client **adidas-Salomon AG**
Designagentur / Designagency **KMS**

Assignment / Briefing: Adidas commissioned us to develop the international opening campaign of the adidas Performance Centres. **Implementation:** We developed the concept "3-STRIPES ARE COMING!", which visualizes the new presence of adidas as the arrival of the three stripes. Posters show scenes of the respective city with oversized adidas stripes running across its buildings and streets.

Meine Models / my models

Aufgabe / Briefing: Gerd George will Art Buyer und Art Directors auf sich aufmerksam machen.
Umsetzung: Die Models von Gerd George sind keine Models. Es sind Leute von der Straße, von nebenan. Darum verschickt er ein Telefonbuch, das wie ein typisches Model-Buch aussieht.

Thema / Subject **model book** • Auftraggeber / Client **Gerd George, Fotograf**
Designagentur / Designagency **Serviceplan, Haus der Kommunikation**

Assignment / Briefing: Gerd George will be regarded by art-buyers and art directors. **Implementation:** The models of Gerd George aren't models. But people on the street, people next door. That's why he sends a telephone directory which looks like a typical model-book.

Rauchring / Smoke Ring

Aufgabe / Briefing: Ziel des Motivs ist es, Aufmerksamkeit zu wecken für die Lebensgefahr, in die Kinder durch Passivrauchen gebracht werden. **Umsetzung:** Über dem Kopf eines kleinen Mädchen steht der Rauchring eines Rauchers wie ein Heiligenschein. Der Heiligenschein assoziiert, dass Kinder, die passiv Zigarettenrauch ausgesetzt werden, dem Himmel – und damit ihrem Tod – schon ein Stück näher sind.

Thema / Subject **Nichtraucher Kampagne, soll vor allem Embrios, Babys und Kinder vor Schäden durch Passivrauchen bewahren / Non-Smoking-Campaign with the aim of preventing damage to embryos, babies and children caused by passive smoking** Auftraggeber / Client **Stiftung Kindergesundheit** Designagentur / Designagency **Serviceplan, Haus der Kommunikation**

Assignment / Briefing: The campaign calls attention to the health risk to children caused through passive smoking. **Implementation:** A smoke ring hangs like a halo over the head of a little girl. The halo associates, that children who are exposed to passive smoking are already a little bit closer to heaven – and therefore closer to death.

getting closer – 100 Jahre RECARO

Aufgabe / Briefing: RECARO ist ein internationaler Hersteller von hochwertigen Autositzen. Der Anlaß „100 Jahre RECARO" sollte genutzt werden, um das Profil der Marke neu zu justieren – Kernkompetenzen und Innovationskraft des Unternehmens/der Marke sollten wieder in den Fokus gerückt werden. Zielgruppe des 4-tägigen Events: Vertreter der internationalen Automobil-Industrie, Lieferanten, Vertreter aus Politik und Wirtschaft, Mitarbeiter. **Umsetzung:** Darstellung von Unternehmensgeschichte und aktuellem Marken-Profil als nach vorne gerichtete Verbindung von Tradition und Innovation. Herausarbeiten der strategischen Kernkompetenzen, um die bisweilen einseitige Wirkung „Recaro = Sport" in Richtung „Recaro = Premium-Produkt" zu korrigieren. Das heißt: Man wollte Geschichte nicht als chronologische Abfolge von Ereignissen darstellen, sondern als Kausalkette, die gleichzeitig auch das Profil des Unternehmens in Gegenwart und Zukunft prägt.

Thema / Subject **Markenbroschüre** • Auftraggeber / Client **Recaro GmbH & Co. KG**
Designagentur / Designagency **Bruce B. GmbH corporate communication**

Assignment / Briefing: RECARO is an international manufacturer of high-quality car seats. The occasion of "100 Years of RECARO" should be utilised to readjust the image of the brand – the core competences and innovative power of the company/brand should be brought back into the forefront. The target group of the 4-day event: representatives of the international automobile industry, suppliers, representatives of politics and business, employees. **Implementation:** Portrayal of the company history and current market profile as a progress-oriented association of tradition and innovation. Elaboration of the strategic core competences to correct the previously one-sided effect of "Recaro = Sport" to become "Recaro = Premium Product". That is to say: There was no desire to portray history as a chronological course of events, but rather as a chain of causes and effects that at the same time will influence the image of the company today as well as in the future.

Stuttgarter Küche – Holzmanufaktur

Aufgabe / Briefing: Der Holzmanufaktur-Showroom befindet sich in unmittelbarer Nähe der Firmen Poggenpohl, bulthaup, SieMatic und Leicht-Küchen. Deshalb sollte ein Werbemittel entwickelt werden, dass sich signifikant von den „Büchern" der Konkurrenz abhebt, aber den gleichen Anspruch und Wertigkeit wiederspiegelt. **Umsetzung:** Fokussierung auf die differenzierenden Merkmale: Persönlichkeit, Nähe, Handarbeit, Regionalität, Individualität. Das heißt: Große Idee statt großes Format, handgemachte Illustration statt Hochglanz-Fotografie, persönliche Ansprache statt Werbe-Gesülze.

Auftraggeber / Client **Holzmanufaktur** • Designagentur / Designagency **Bruce B. GmbH**

Assignment / Briefing: The wooden factory showroom is located directly near the firms Poggenpohl, bulthaup, SieMatic and Leicht-Küchen. Thus, an advertising means should be developed that stands out significantly from the "books" of the competition yet reflects the same level of demand and quality. **Implementation:** A focus on differentiating characteristics: personality, proximity, handicraft, regionality, and individuality. In other words: Big ideas instead of a big format, hand-made illustrations instead of high-gloss photography, addressing people personally instead of with advertising babble.

argonauten G2 Corporate Website

Aufgabe / Briefing: Die Düsseldorfer Multichannel-Agentur argonauten360° hat sich zum 1. September 2006 dem internationalen G2 Network angeschlossen. Zum gleichen Termin änderte sich auch der Firmenname in argonauten G2 und damit der Gesamtauftritt der argonauten. Als elementarer Bestandteil des neuen Auftritts galt es eine Website zu entwickeln - diese sollte zum einen des neuen CD's in Anlehnung an das G2 Network entsprechen und zum anderen sowohl die argonauten, so wie sie sich selbst wahrnehmen und auch von außen wahrgenommen werden wollen, als auch die Expertise der argonauten im Onlinebereich widerspiegeln. URL: http://www.argonautenG2.de

Umsetzung: Der neue Internetauftritt ermöglicht dem User eine direkte Interaktion mit den argonauten selbst, die in Form von Protagonisten, durch integrierte Videosequenzen dargestellt, auf der Website agieren. Durch die Live-argonauten bekommt der User tatsächlich das Gefühl argonauten G2 – sowohl als Unternehmen als auch die Mitarbeiter selbst – kennen zu lernen. Der User taucht durch die innovative Navigation und die spannenden Darstellungsformen in die Welt der argonauten G2 ein.

Thema / Subject **argonauten G2** • Auftraggeber / Client **argonauten G2 GmbH**
Designagentur / Designagency **argonauten G2 GmbH**

Assignment / Briefing: The Dusseldorf-based multi-channel agency argonauten360° joined the international G2 Network on September 1, 2006. On the same date, the company changed its name to argonauten G2 and also introduced its new brand identity. It was essential to develop a website as an elementary part of the new identity. This was to correspond to the new CD, which was based on that of the G2 Network. At the same time, it was important to convey how argonauten perceives itself as a company and wishes to be viewed by the public. Reflecting argonauten's expertise in online media was also a major requirement. **Implementation:** The new website allows users to interact directly with argonauten in the form of characters who appear on the website in integrated video sequences. The live argonauten figures allow users to find out more about argonauten G2 – both the company and the employees themselves. The innovative navigation elements and exciting types of visualization allow users to experience the world of argonauten G2.

Federleicht

Aufgabe / Briefing: Was nicht kommuniziert wird, existiert nicht. Mit dem Mailing „Ein federleichtes Dankeschön" will der Absender seine Stakeholder über erhaltene Auszeichnungen informieren, ohne sich mit fremden Federn zu schmücken. **Umsetzung:** Ein federleichtes Kommunikationsinstrument, das die Richtigkeit Multatuli's Aufforderung „Suchet den Inhalt, und die Form wird euch zugeworfen" mit großer Leichtigkeit unter Beweis stellt.

Thema / Subject **Mailing** • Auftraggeber / Client **Teunen Konzepte GmbH**
Designagentur / Designagency **Heine/Lenz/Zizka**

Assignment / Briefing: If it is not communicated, it does not exist. In mailing his "Feather Light Thank You" the sender wants to inform his clients and supporters about awards received without covering himself in false glory. **Implementation:** Using an instrument of communication as light as a feather proves with its tremendous lightness the rightness of Multatuli's challenge to "Seek the content and you will be tossed the form."

Nano Maca

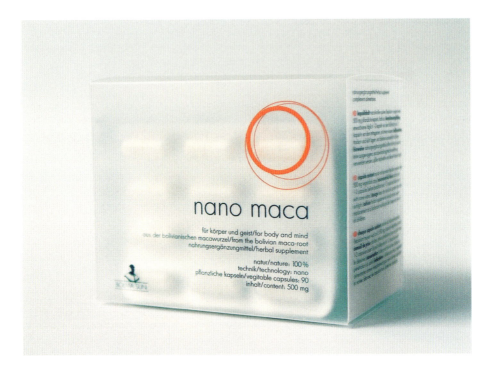

Aufgabe / Briefing: Nano Maca ist ein energiesteigerndes Nahrungsergänzungsmittel aus der bolivianischen Maca-Wurzel, dass unter Einsatz der Nano-Technologie seine Wirkung erhöht. Die Vermarktung ist auf entsprechend hohem Level angesiedelt. Job: Marke, Claim, Verpackung
Umsetzung: Nano Maca wurde als Wellness-Produkt im gehobenen Preissegment positioniert. Die Designstrategie setzte dabei auf eine pharmazeutisch-kosmetische Kombination. Auf tradiertes Design der Inka-Kultur wurde bewußt verzichtet und lediglich das Symbol der Sonne abstrakt aufgegriffen.

Thema / Subject **Marke, Claim und Verpackungsdesign für ein Nahrungsergänzungsmittel**
Auftraggeber / Client **Eco Terra GmbH** • Produktdesign / Productdesign **Eiche, Oehjne Design**

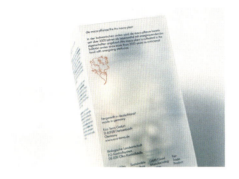

Assignment / Briefing: Nano Maca is an energy delivering herbal supplement made of the bolivian maca root. The also new nano-technology promises a profound effect guarantee due to the higher fragmentation of the core product. Job: Brand, claim and packaging Development. **Implementation:** The strategic solution consisted in diverging from the common and known outer packaging design for herbal supplement by giving the product a wellness-positioning by combining the looks of pharmaceutics of cosmetics. The brand abstained from the commonly used ways of representing the inca-culture. Their outstanding significance of the sun though, has been included to the brand in an abstract way.

stand up

Aufgabe / Briefing: Schaffung eines multifunktionalen Klapp-Stehtisches, mobil, für unterschiedliche Einsatzzwecke, objektgeeignete Ausführung, funktional. **Umsetzung:** Kombination bewährter Bauteile und innovativer Technik, individuell bedruckbare Tischoberflächen, Platz sparende Aufbewahrung, neu entwickeltes Prinzip (Patent) des Einklappens in nicht gekannter Perfektion, verringertes Tischgewicht, gute Standfestigkeit.

Thema / Subject **Klapp-Stehtisch** • Auftraggeber / Client **Hiller Objektmöbel** Designagentur / Designagency **.molldesign**

Assignment / Briefing: Development of a functional as well as aesthetical folding bar table for versatile applications. **Implementation:** Folding bar table with ingenious functions and details, you don't have to hide underneath a table cloth. The application of approved components and innovative technology ensures a fast, simple and safe handling, solid stand in spite of a low weight and a less demand of storeroom.

Posterbroschüre Irina „IRA" Kalentieva

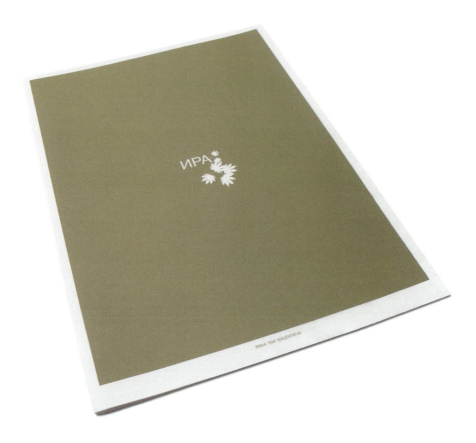

Aufgabe / Briefing: Entwicklung einer A2-Posterbroschüre für die erfolgreiche russische Mountainbikerin Irina „IRA" Kalentieva **Umsetzung:** „IRA" Kalentieva steht für fahrerisches Können in anspruchsvollem Gelände. Daher wurde die Gestaltung durch großzügigen Einsatz von Fläche, Typografie, Fotografie bewusst hochwertig gehalten. Die metallische Schmuckfarbe dient zur Veredelung. Illustrationen schaffen eine Verbindung zur Ursprünglichkeit des Geländes.

Thema / Subject **Entwicklung einer Posterbroschüre** • Auftraggeber / Client **RTI Sports GmbH**
Designagentur / Designagency **KW43 BRANDDESIGN**

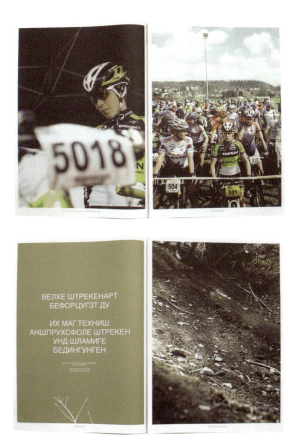

Assignment / Briefing: Developing of a DIN A2 poster-broschure for the succesful Russian mountain-biker Irina "IRA" Kalentieva **Implementation:** "IRA" Kalentieva stands for driving competence in challenging area. Therefore the design was consciously held on a high-class level by the generous use of surface, typography and photography. The metallic spot colour serves for refinement. Illustrations create a connection to the nativeness of the area.

Claus Koch™ Eigenanzeige / ADC Buch

Aufgabe / Briefing: Eigenanzeige mit Bezug zum ADC Buch Kleben bleiben (Kaugummis).
Umsetzung: Foto und Inhalt wie Thema des Buches. (Kommunikation, die kleben bleibt. In den Köpfen der Menschen. Kommunikation, die eine andere Konsistenz, Farbe, Geschmacksrichtung hat. Kommunikation, die eine runde Sache ist, die Spaß macht. Kommunikation, die auch nach mehrmaligem Kauen nicht an Geschmack verliert.)

Auftraggeber / Client **Claus Koch**™ • Designagentur / Designagency **Claus Koch**™

Assignment / Briefing: Advertisement with regards to the ADC Book „Chewinggum".
Implementation: Motive and text as theme of the book. (Communication that sticks – in people's minds. Communication that has a different consistency, colour and taste. Communication that is well-rounded and fun. Communication that doesn't lose its taste even after being chewed several times.)

Frischzelle / Live-cell

Aufgabe / Briefing: Publikationsserie für die Ausstellungsreihe „Frischzelle", die junge Künstler im Kunstmuseum Stuttgart zeigt. **Umsetzung:** Die Broschüren wahren einerseits den Gesamtzusammenhang der Serie, geben jedem Künstler aber auch die Möglichkeit individueller Gestaltung. Format, Ausstattung, Typografie, sowie ein beigefügter Bogen mit Klebebildchen aus der Ausstellung bleiben bei allen Ausgaben gleich.

Thema / Subject **Ausstellungsbroschüren** • Auftraggeber / Client **Stiftung Kunstmuseum Stuttgart GmbH** • Designagentur / Designagency **L2M3 Kommunikationsdesign GmbH**

Assignment / Briefing: Publication series for the exhibition series "Live-cell" that shows young artists in the Stuttgart Art Museum. **Implementation:** On the one hand, the brochures preserve the coherence of the entire series, on the other hand they also provide each artist with the opportunity to express himself on an individual basis. Format, layout, typography as well as an enclosed sheet with stickers from the exhibition stay the same for all editions.

Redesign Corporate Website Wormland

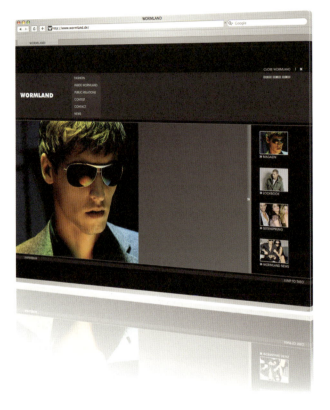

Aufgabe / Briefing: Für „WORMLAND – der Men's Fashion Spezialist" sollte ein Redesign der Website vorgenommen werden. Agonist media wurde mit der Aufgabe bedacht eine Site zu entwickeln, die sich vordergründig als saisonaler modischer „Teaser" versteht. Hintergründig aber die Marke WORMLAND und Ihre Fashion-Kompetenz kommuniziert. **Umsetzung:** Agonist media entwickelte für WORMLAND eine Website mit einem klar strukturierten Design, einer innovativen Navigation, einer eigens für Wormland entwickelten „dynamic sidebar", die für den User mit unterschiedlichsten Content aufwartet. Darüber hinaus verfügt die Website über einen eigenen Mediaplayer, der sowohl Video- wie Audiofiles abspielt.

Thema / Subject **Website** • Auftraggeber / Client **THEO WORMLAND GmbH & Co.KG**
Designagentur / Designagency **Agonist media: agency for advertisement**

Assignment / Briefing: "WORMLAND – the men's fashion specialist" requested a Redesign of their website. Agonist media was asked to visualize a website which would be recognized as a seasonal fashion teaser in the foreground, but undernath the site would mainly communicate WORMLAND as the brand and its fahion competencies. **Implementation:** Agonist media developed a website for WORMLAND with a clear cut design, a cutting-edge navigation menu, a "dynamic sidebar" with a large variety of different content and in addition to that the website offers an own mediaplayer, which plays back audio file as well video files.

Redesign Corporate Packaging AESKU

Aufgabe / Briefing: Entwicklung eines neuen Verpackungsdesigns für die AESKU.DIAGNOSTICS, die zweien Ihrer Produktlinien ein neueres, zeitgemäßeres Image verleihen sollten. Vordergründig sollte das neue Verpackungsdesign potenzielle neue Kunden auf der Messe anlocken. Hintergründig sollte die neue Corporate Identity kommuniziert und die Verkaufszahlen der Produkte erhöht werden.
Umsetzung: Die zentralen Farben der neuen AESKU Verpackungen lehnen sich im Grundsatz an die Wort-Bildmarke der AESKU.DIAGNOSTICS an, wobei ein intensiveres Grün als Lead-colour hinzugefügt wurde. Zusätzlich wurde eine organische Form in das Konzept aufgenommen. Diese erlaubt vielseitige Interpretationsmöglichkeiten, wobei sie eine Symbiose zwischen Natur, Technik und Heilung anmuten lassen soll.

Thema / Subject **Verpackung** • Auftraggeber / Client **AESKU.DIAGNOSTICS**
Designagentur / Designagency **Agonist media: agency for advertisement**

Assignment / Briefing: AESKU.DIAGNOSTICS asked Agonist media to redesign two of their corporate packages. Primarily the new contemporary package design should attract new customers on exhibition fairs and increase the sales figures of the products. Secondly the new package should communicate the new corporate identity of AESKU.DIAGNOSTICS **Implementation:** The main colours of the new AESKU packages are evolved form the corporate logo of AESKU.DIAGNOSTICS, whereas one more intense light green colour was added as a lead colour. Additionally the concept was extended with an organic shape which should symbolize a symbiosis between nature, engineering and healing.

Ausstellungskatalog „Alessandro Carloni – Sketchbooks"

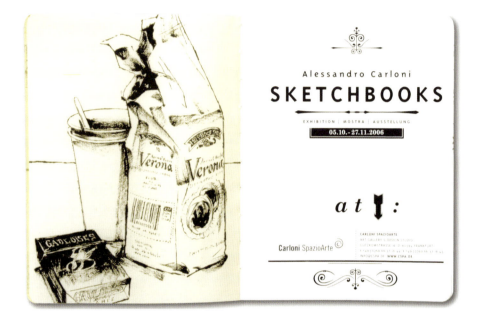

Aufgabe / Briefing: Alessandro Carloni arbeitet als Storykünstler und Animation Supervisor für Dreamworks Animation Studios in Hollywood. In seiner Freizeit zeichnet er in seinen Moleskine-Skizzenbüchern. Zum Anlass seiner Ausstellung sollte ein Katalog erstellt werden. **Umsetzung:** Gestalterische Anlehnung des Ausstellungskataloges an die Moleskine-Skizzenbücher, die der Künstler benutzt (schwarzes Cover, abgerundete Ecken, 2-Farbdruck schwarz/gelb, Elastikband).

Thema / Subject **Ausstellungskatalog** • Auftraggeber / Client **Carloni SpazioArte**
Designagentur / Designagency **Carloni SpazioArte**

Assignment / Briefing: Alessandro Carloni works as a Story Artist and Animation Supervisor for Dreamworks Animation Studios in Hollywood. In his spare time he makes sketches in his Moleskine notebooks. On the occasion of his exhibition a catalogue was to be designed. **Implementation:** The design of the exhibition catalogue utilises formal elements of the Moleskine notebooks that the artist uses (black cover, rounded edges, 2 color print in black and yellow, elastic).

AWARD

**Wanderausstellung der International School of Stuttgart /
Travelling Exhibition of the International School of Stuttgart**

Aufgabe / Briefing: Zum 20-jährigen Jubiläum wurde für die International School of Stuttgart eine Ausstellung geplant. Mit knappem Budget sollte ein hoher Kommunikationswert in der Öffentlichkeit erreicht werden. Die Wanderausstellung wurde bisher an verschiedenen Orten im Großraum Stuttgart gezeigt, und erfreut sich einer sehr guten Reputation in der Informationskommunikation an die Öffentlichkeit. **Umsetzung:** Das Leporello dokumentiert das Konzept, die Bespielung der Ausstellungsorte und die entwickelten Werbemedien zu diesem Projekte. Wir kommunizieren die spürbare Besonderheit in der Art, Philosophie und Anwendung der Identität dieser wertvollen Bildungseinrichtung.

Assignment / Briefing: The exhibition was planned for the International School of Stuttgart as a part of their celebration of the school's 20th birthday. The goal was to achieve a high level of communication to the public on a limited budget. The traveling exhibition has thus far been on display at various locations throughout the greater Stuttgart area and has gained a very good reputation as an information communication medium. **Implementation:** Details of the exhibition concept, the exploitation of the exhibition locations and the materials developed for the project are documented in the Leporello submission. We have communicated the tangible distinctiveness of the approach, philosophy and identity of this invaluable educational establishment.

Thema / Subject **Ausstellungsgestaltung und Kommunikationsmedien** • Auftraggeber / Client
International School of Stuttgart e.V. • Designagentur / Designagency **Engenhart Visuelle Kommunikation, Lothar Bertrams (Fotograf DGPh)**

**GUTE GESTALTUNG.
DER WETTBEWERB DES DDC FÜR
JEDES JAHR NEU.**

Informationen zu finden unter www.ddc.de

ALLE GESTALTUNGSBEREICHE.

www.ddc.de

INSTANT 63 - Ménage à trois

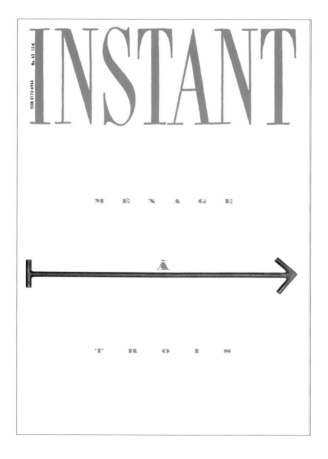

Aufgabe / Briefing: Medirata – Agentur für Kommunikation in Freiburg – will das 10jährige Jubiläum mit einer Kunst-Aktion feiern. Inhalt Kultur und Kommunikation sind nicht zu trennen.
Umsetzung: Die Agentur feiert nicht sich, sondern 3 Künstler (Leipzig, München, Rüsselsheim) an 3 Tagen in einer klassischen Galerie: Vernissage, Midissage, Finissage mit einem Kunstkatalog der anderen Art – INSTANT – Ménage à trois.

Thema / Subject **Ausstellungskatalog**
Auftraggeber / Client **Medirata, Agentur für Kommunikation GmbH**
Designagentur / Designagency **Agentur für feine Werbung**

Assignment / Briefing: Medirata – an agency for communication in Freiburg – intends to celebrate its 10th anniversary with an art show. Content: culture and communication are inseparable.
Implementation: The agency is celebrating not itself, but three artists (Leipzig, Munich, Rüsselsheim) on 3 days in a classical gallery: vernissage, midissage, finissage with an art catalogue that's rather different – INSTANT – Ménage à trois.

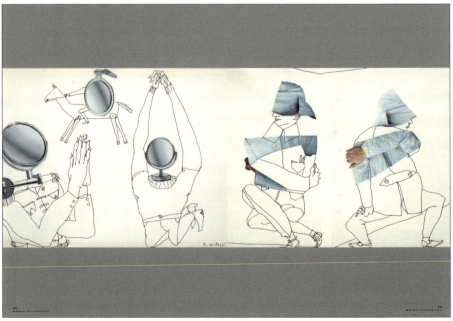

„Instrumente"

Make the road a concert hall

Aufgabe / Briefing: Aufgabe war es, die Bekanntheit des belgischen Yamaha Vertragshändlers in Deuschland zu steigern. **Umsetzung:** Die Kampagne zeigt, welch schönen Sound man mit Auspuff-Anlagen von Yamaha Racing erreichen kann. Das Spiel mit der Verwechslung ist gewollt – Musikinstrument und Motorrad haben schließlich denselben Hersteller: den japanischen Konzern Yamaha.

Thema / Subject **Yamaha Racing** • Auftraggeber / Client **Lux AG** • Designagentur / Designagency **Y&R Germany**

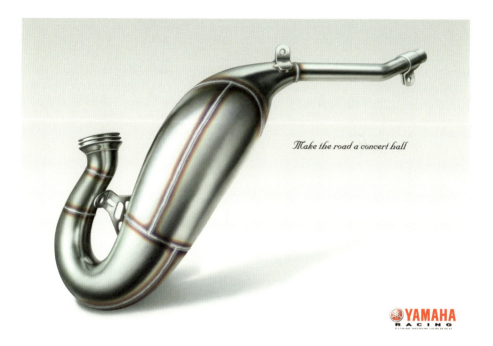

Assignment / Briefing: Task was to raise awareness of the Belgian Yamaha motorcycle dealership in Germany. **Implementation:** The campaign shows that you can generate beautiful sounds with Yamaha racing exhaust parts and any associations with Yamaha's musical instruments are absolutely desired.

house rebels

Aufgabe / Briefing: Gestaltung einer – schnell wieder erkennbaren – Identität für eine House Music CD Serie. **Umsetzung:** Einen nicht unwesentlichen Beitrag zum Erfolg der mittlerweile zum Kult avancierten House CD Serie, leistete die auf einer simplen Idee basierende Gestaltung: Während auf dem Cover eine stets unbekannte Schönheit dem DJ-Mix der (ehemals) gleichnamigen Radiosendung frönt, zeigt die Rückseite lediglich das Radio. Dabei tritt die Typographie dezent in den Hintergrund und läßt der unprätentiösen Fotografie den Vortritt.

Thema / Subject **Visual Identity / CD-Serie „house rebels 001-011"** • Auftraggeber / Client
7 Lux Entertainment • Designagentur / Designagency **BORSELLINO & CO.**

Assignment / Briefing: Design a – fast recognizable – identity for a house music CD series.
Implementation: For the by now very popular house CD series, the design, which is based on a simple idea, made a not unessentially contribution to its success: While an unknown beauty on the cover is indulged to the DJ mix of the (formerly) same name called radio show, the back is showing only the radio. The typography is staying discreet in the background, while giving precedence to the unpretentiously photography.

BEYOND

RESTAURANT
LOUNGE
TAKE AWAY

Aufgabe / Briefing: Entwicklung eines Namens und einer visuellen Identität für ein Restaurant (mit zusätzlicher Lounge und Take Away). **Umsetzung:** Beyond Restaurant, Beyond Lounge, Beyond Take Away – ein Name der mit nur einem Wort das Leitbild der angestrebten Unternehmenskultur ausdrückt und zugleich als Werbeaussage dient. Und mit „Beyond Wine" oder „Beyond Cooking" zudem erweiterbar auf alle erdenklichen PR-Events wie Weinabende und Kochkurse ist. Visuell wird dieser hohe Anspruch durch einen konsequenten Illustrationsstil transportiert: Marktmotive, frische Zutaten also, welche die Basis des tagtäglichen kulinarischen Schaffens bilden. In Kombination mit diesen Schlüsselmotiven fungiert das flexible Signet, ohne sich an starre Farbvorgaben halten zu müssen, als „Etikett" und somit als Absender.

Thema / Subject **Namensentwicklung und Corporate Design / BEYOND Restaurant**
Auftraggeber / Client **Plasse Project GmbH** • Designagentur / Designagency **BORSELLINO & CO.**
Illustration **Mone Maurer**

Assignment / Briefing: Brand development and visual identity for a restaurant (with additional lounge and take away section). **Implementation:** Beyond Restaurant, Beyond Lounge, Beyond Take Away – a name that in only one word expresses the mission statement and in the same the slogan. And moreover with "Beyond Wine" and "Beyond Cooking" is expandable to all imaginable sorts of PR events as wine or cookery courses. Visually this high demand is transported by a strong illustrational style: market place images, therefore fresh ingredients, which day in, day out are the basics of culinary work. In combination with these key visuals the flexible logo act as a label, without following rigid colour codes, and thus as sender.

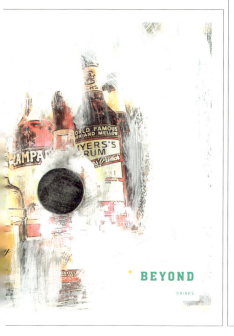

JURYVORSITZ UND ORGANISATION DER JURYSITZUNG

Vorsitz der Gesamtjury / Chair of the Entire Jury

Organisation

Thomas Feicht
Präsident des DDC / President of the DDC

Susanne Hoffmann
DDC Office

JURY RAUM

Organisation

»Der ideale Prater für Frankfurt.« / »The ideal Big Wheel for Frankfurt.«

Anne Deile
DDC Office

Dieter Ludwig
zu / on KUNST I RAD

»Architektonisch stark genug, ohne ein Gebäude zu sein zeigt er mit geringsten Mitteln ein überzeugendes Raumkonzept. Das Licht ist perfekt inszeniert. Lobenswert ist der Mut des Auftraggebers!« / »Architecturally strong enough, without being a building, and with minimalist elegance exhibits a persuasively aesthetic spatial concept. The light has been perfectly staged. All credit to the client's boldness!«

»Ein Projekt macht eine Reise durch die Disziplinen und Jurys. Es lässt sich nicht eingrenzen und gewinnt zum Schluss dort, wo es herkam, im Bereich Raum, eine Bronzemedaille.« / »A project makes its way through the disciplines and juries. It defies any attempt at classification and ultimately wins a bronze medal where it came from, in the space category.«

Hans-Ulrich von Mende
zu / on U-BAHNHOF LOHRING, Bochum

Laurent Lacour
zu / on PRO-SAFE IAA 2005

JURY IMAGE

»Inszenierte Modefotografie in Verbindung mit natürlicher Anmutung der Akteure ist die besondere fotografische Leistung dieses Bandes. Verarbeitung der Extraklasse!« / »Perfectly staged fashion photography in conjunction with the natural elegance of the protagonists is the particular artistic merit of this volume. Exceptional workmanship!«

»Endlich konnte ich meiner Frau einmal erklären, was gute Designer ausmacht.« / »At last I could explain to my wife what makes a good designer.«

Pancho Ballweg
zu / on ONGWE – Der Leopard

Niko Gültig
zu / on 10 JAHRE A&W-DESIGNER DES JAHRES

»Im klassischen Sujet des Stilllebens verbindet Melting Pot das Abstrakte mit dem Opulenten, das Erhabene mit dem Banalen, das Ewige mit dem Vergänglichen.« / »In the classical subject of still life Melting Pot marries the abstract to the opulent, the exalted to the banal, the eternal to the transient.«

»Jedes Motiv erzählt eine spannende Geschichte. Einfach genial.« / »Each motif tells an exciting story. A work of genius.«

Bernhard Franken
zu / on MELTING POT

Peter Heßler
zu / on SZ KRIMI-BIBLIOTHEK

**JURY
PRODUKT**

»Eine fantastische Materialstruktur in Verbindung mit puristischem Design lässt eine hochklassige Synthese entstehen. Die trotz der silbernen Hülle Gold verdient.« / »A fantastic material structure in conjunction with purist design creates a superlative synthesis, which despite the silver exterior truly deserves gold.«

»Wenn ich als abstürzender Passagier einen Wunsch frei hätte – ich würde gerne dieses Löschfahrzeug kommen sehen.« / »If as a crash-landing passenger I were granted one wish – I'd like to see this fire-engine coming.«

Holger Diehl
zu / on ALCOM SERIES

Gordon Levine
zu / on ROSENBAUER PANTHER

»Ich finde das Produkt gut, weil es eine wunderbare, zeitgemässe Umsetzung der Weihnachtszeremonie für die mobile Gesellschaft zeigt.« / »I think this is a good product, because it shows a wonderful, contemporary version of the Christmas ceremony for the mobile society.«

»Und wieder eine überzeugend einfache Lösung.« / »And once again a persuasively simple solution.«

Gunter Neuhaus
zu / on iPRAY

Peter Oehjne
zu / on TRICK STICK

JURY DIGITAL

»Ich liebe das Meer.« / »I love the sea.«

»Eine hervorragend integrierte Kommunikationslösung von Film, Fotografie und Text. Die Website ist ein gelungener Appetizer für das Buch.« / »An excellently integrated communication solution featuring film, photography and text. The website is a successful appetiser for the book.«

Rainer Gehrisch
zu / on PLANET MEER

Isolde Pech
zu / on PASSIONists

»Designpassionist!!!« / »Design passionist!!!«

»Extrem charmant und dabei ganz einfach. Man taucht in eine andere Welt.« / »Extremely charming and yet very simple. You're immersed in a different world.«

Claus Krogmann
zu / on PASSIONists

Gregor Ade
zu / on PLANET MEER

JURY NETZWERK

»Einfach gute Gestaltung!« / »Simply good design!«

»We felt the adventure.«

Till Melchior
zu / on WWW.HUNDERTHUNDERT.COM

Heike Brockmann
zu / on MOTOCROSS Journalism Adventure

»Das Projekt zeigt gesellschaftspolitisches Bewusstsein. Eine Landschaft wird als Erholungsgebiet für den Menschen erhalten. Der Park macht Naturphänomene sinnlich erlebbar.« / »The project shows socio-political awareness. A landscape is preserved as a leisure area for humankind. The park enables natural phenomena to be experienced as sensory percepts.«

»Features und future werden auf intelligente Weise zum Gesamterlebnis.« / »Features and future are intelligently fused into an experiential whole.«

Katrin Hupe
zu / on WETTERPARK OFFENBACH

Michael Eibes
zu / on MOTOCROSS Journalism Adventure

»Ein kreativer, intelligenter Event mit spielerischer Qualität, der eine hohe Attraktivität und Aktivierungspotential bewirkt. Eine gelungene Synthese aus eigenständigem Eventauftritt bei gleichzeitig klarer Anbindung an die Dachmarke.« / »A creative, intelligent event with playful quality ensures a high level of attractiveness and activation potential. A successful synthesis of an autonomous event with a simultaneously clear link to the family brand.«

Prof. Rüdiger Goetz
zu / on MOTOCROSS Journalism Adventure

»Die Ausstellung im Fokus der Fußballweltmeisterschaft ist monumental inszeniert ohne distanzierte Denkmalhaftigkeit. Sie verbindet Information und Interaktion.« / »The exhibition in the focus of the World Cup is monumentally staged without aloof monumentalism. It fuses information with interaction.«

Beate Steil
zu / on WALK OF IDEAS

**JURY
ZUKUNFT**

»Neue Briefmarken braucht das Land!« / »This country needs new stamps!«

»Macht neugierig, fantasievoll, Fernweh!« / »Triggers curiosity, imagination, wanderlust!«

Prof. Gregor Krisztian
zu / on NEUE BRIEFMARKEN
FÜR DEUTSCHLAND

Vera Uchytil
zu / on FERNE, FORTBEWEGUNG, FREMDE

»Hat Biss!« / »Has bite!«

»Ich empfehle: In Bewegung bleiben.« / »I recommend: keep moving.«

Till Schneider
zu / on AN APPLE A DAY

Dirk Brömmel
zu / on GRINGOGRAFICO –
zwei Designer auf der Walz

Wo sind die neuen Gestalter/innen? Womit beschäftigen sie sich? Wie vermitteln sie ihre Ideen?
In der Kategorie Zukunft des DDC-Wettbewerbs sind 68 Beiträge eingereicht worden, die darauf Antworten geben können. Student/innen und Absolvent/innen haben sich von der Produktentwicklung, über die Unternehmenskommunikation und Informationsvermittlung bis hin zur persönlichen Standortbestimmung dabei vielfältige und vielschichtige Gedanken zu ihrer Umwelt und ihrer eigenen Haltung dazu gemacht. In der Spritzigkeit der konzeptionellen Ansätze, in der Konsequenz bei der Umsetzung sowie in der professionellen Form der Präsentation ist zu einem Großteil Außergewöhnliches sichtbar geworden. Schön zu beobachten, wie breit der Bogen sich von der akribischen Untersuchung des absolut Alltäglichen bis zur experimentellen Dokumentation der eigenen Erfahrungen spannt. Wenn diese Arbeiten ein repräsentativer Schnitt durch das darstellen, was momentan an den Hochschulen geleistet wird, muss man sich um die Zukunft der Gestaltung aus dieser Sicht keine Sorgen machen. **Till Schneider, DDC**

ZUKUNFT

Where are the new designers? What are they working on? How are they communicating their ideas? In the "Future" category of the DDC Competition, 68 entries were submitted that might help to answer these questions. Students and graduates have come up with multifaceted, multilayered thoughts on their perceptual/conceptual environment and their response to it, ranging from product development and corporate communication and informational efficacy to personal self-analysis. In the sparkling freshness of the conceptual approaches adopted, in the stringency of execution, and the professionalism of the presentation, a goodly portion of exceptional talent is manifested. It is gratifying to observe how broad the spectrum is, from meticulous examinations of the quintessentially quotidian to experimental documentation of individual experience. If these works constitute a representative cross-section of what is currently being achieved at university level, we need have no worries about the future of design excellence. **Till Schneider, DDC**

Gringografico – Zwei Designer auf der Walz

Aufgabe / Briefing: Was passiert, wenn zwei Grafikdesign-Studenten, inspiriert durch die Zimmermanns-Walz, für ein halbes Jahr in die Ferne ziehen und zwischen Kanada und Peru auf ungewöhnliche Jobsuche gehen? **Umsetzung:** Ein Roadbook über 17.000 km Straße mit Momentaufnahmen aus dem Alltag zweier Grafik-Gesellen und lebensnahen Erfahrungsberichten zwischen Arbeit und Abenteuer.

Thema / Subject **Roadbook** • Diplomanden / Diploma Candidates **Benjamin Bartels, Maximilian Kohler** • Hochschule / University **Fachhochschule Wiesbaden** • Betreuender Professor / Advisory Professor **Prof. Dieter Fröbisch, Prof. Christine Wagner**

Assignment / Briefing: What happens when two graphic design students, inspired by an old tradition called the "Walz", take to the road and look for work along the way between Canada and Peru? **Implementation:** A roadbook about over 10.000 miles of highway with snap-shots of the everyday life of two graphic-journeymen and stories about work and wanderlust.

SILBER

An apple a day ...

Umsetzung: Der Apfel dient als Stellvertreter, um über unseren Umgang mit Alltäglichem nachzudenken. Das Buch thematisiert die Begriffe Wert und Verantwortung und die Möglichkeit ihrer Visualisierung. Politische, ethische, geschichtliche, wirtschaftliche und poetische Aspekte kommen in Bildergeschichten, Grafiken und Texten zum Ausdruck und laden zur genauen Betrachtung ein.

Thema / Subject **Buch** • Diplomand / Diploma Candidate **Isabell Zirbeck** • Hochschule / University **Hochschule für Künste Bremen** • Betreuender Professor / Advisory Professor **Prof. Andrea Rauschenbusch**

Implementation: The apple serves as a representative that makes us think about our dealing with everyday-life. The central theme of the book are the terms „value" and „responsibility" and how these can be visualized. Political, ethical, historical, economical and poetical aspects are shown in picture stories, graphics and texts and call for an in-depth reflection.

FABSTUDIO

Aufgabe / Briefing: Welche Chancen und Möglichkeiten bieten sich für Designer, Hersteller und Kunden bei der „Individuellen Serienproduktion"? Wie ließen sich diese in einem Konzept umsetzen?
Umsetzung: Theoretische Auseinandersetzung: „Kunde-Designer-Hersteller"-Beziehung, generative Herstellungsverfahren, Metadesign von Lampenschirmen, Entwurf eines software basierten Konfigurators (FABSTUDIO) zu Manipulation der Metadesigns durch den Prosumenten (= Konsument + Produzent).

Thema / Subject **Individualisierung von Serienprodukten / Individualisation of Mass Products**
Diplomand / Diploma Candidate **Jan Christian Delfs** • Hochschule / University **Muthesius Kunsthochschule Kiel** • Betreuende Professoren/ Advisory Professors **Prof. Ulrich Hirsch**

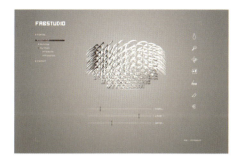

Assignment / Briefing: What are the opportunities and potentials of "individual mass production" for designers, producers and customers? How could they be realised in a conceptualisation?
Implementation: Theoretical discussion about "Customer- designer-producer"-Relationship and generative production processes, metadesign of lampshades, Design of a software-based configurator (FABSTUDIO) that allows manipulation of metadesigns by prosumers (= consumers + producers).

speck,kremin: 40 stunden design / speck,kremin: 40h design

Aufgabe / Briefing: Die Dokumentation eines Designexperiments am lebenden Objekt. Als finalen Realitätsabgleich akquirieren wir startup-Unternehmen und stellen ihnen unentgeltlich jeweils 40 Stunden Arbeitskraft für Designleistungen zur Verfügung. Dabei dokumentieren wir, was nach 4,5 Jahren Designstudium bei der Bewältigung täglicher Designaufgaben umgesetzt und kommuniziert werden kann. **Umsetzung:** Der Designprozess, die -argumentation sowie die Abwicklung jeder einzelnen Aufgabe werden vom ersten Kundenkontakt bis zur finalen Übergabe auf unserer Website offengelegt. Die Kunden können online jeden Entwicklungsschritt mitverfolgen, nachvollziehen und sich dadurch in den Designprozess einbringen. Am Ende des Diplomprojekts wird der Verlauf der einzelnen Projekte in den Kontext der von uns gemachten Erfahrungen gesetzt und in einer abschliessenden Printdokumentation zusammengefasst.

Thema / Subject **Dokumentation** • Diplomanden / Diploma Candidates **Dominic Speck, Daniel Kremin** • Hochschule / University **Fachhochschule Düsseldorf, Fachbereich Design** • Betreuende Professoren / Advisory Professors **Prof. Philipp Teufel, Dominik Mycielski**

Assignment / Briefing: Documentation of a design experiment as work in progress. To get a final reality-check we approach start-up enterprises and supply them with 40 working hours as designers – free of charge. During this span of time we reveal, what can be put into every-day-practice and communicated after a 4,5 years' education in design. **Implementation:** We make the design process, the design reasoning as well as the execution of every single design task tranparent on our website. From the first contact with the customer to the final handing out of the results. Being online the customers can trace the development of the work step by step and they can get involved in the design process as well. At the end of the diploma we regard the development of the single projects in the context of the experiences we made. All results are collected and displayed in a print-documentation.

INDEX

INDEX

GRAND PRIX

Seite 10-21

AUDI AG

Audi. Vorsprung entsteht zuerst im Kopf.

Audi. Excellence starts in the creative mind.

GOLD

Seite 25-29

Titel
MotoCross Journalism Adventure

Auftraggeber
**Leipziger & Partner PR GmbH,
Jürg W. Leipziger,
Martin Gehl**

Designagentur
Another ROMEOTM Design

Creative Direction
Oliver Daxenbichler

Art Direction
Matthias Scherer

Text
**Marijana Condic
Laura Nolte**

Kundenberater
**Laura Nolte
Marijana Condic**

DTP-Studio
Another ROMEOTM Design

Multimediaagentur
Maguro:Agentur

Web Design
Another ROMEOTM Design

Flash Composing
**Another ROMEOTM Design /
Maguro:Agentur**

Programmierung
**J. M. Tec GmbH /
Maguro:Agentur**

Videoproduktion
Another ROMEOTM Design

SILBER

Seite 32-33

Titel
Adidas GMM Locker Room

Thema / Produkt
Sportartikel / Instant Showroom

Auftraggeber
**Adidas Salomon AG,
Herr Chris Aubrey**

Designagentur
Mutabor Design GmbH

Creative Direction
Heinrich Paravicini

Art Direction
Christian Tönsmann

Kundenberater
Christian Tönsmann

Programmierung
Stephan Huber

Videoproduktion
**Electric Umbrella,
Jens-Eric Peter**

Illustration
**Steffen Mackert
Michael Bamber
Christoph Zielke
Kristina Düllmann**

Fotografie
Diverse

Innenarchitektur
**Mutabor Design GmbH,
Frederike Putz**

Seite 34-35

Titel
**Voraus denken.
Mercedes-Benz auf der
IAA Frankfurt 2005.**

Thema / Produkt
Messeauftritt

Auftraggeber
**DaimlerChrysler AG,
Stuttgart**

Kommunikation
**Atelier Markgraph GmbH,
Frankfurt am Main**

Architektur
**Kauffmann Theilig &
Partner Freie
Architekten BDA,
Ostfildern**

Lichtdesign
**TLD Planungsgruppe,
Wendlingen**

Grafikdesign
**Design Hoch Drei,
Stuttgart**

Messebau
**Ernst F. Ambrosius &
Sohn, Frankfurt am Main**

BRONZE

Seite 38-41

Titel
Wetterpark Offenbach

Thema / Produkt
Wetterpark

Auftraggeber
Planungsverband Ballungsraum Rhein-Main, Stadt Offenbach, DWD

Verantwortlich
Beate Schwarz
Hanne Münster-Voswinkel
Ulrike Rupprecht

Konzeption / Design / Architektur
unit-design

Konzeption / Creative Direction
Bernd Hilpert,
Peter Eckart

Exponat- und Informationsdesign
Heidrun Althen,
Robert Cristinetti,
Peter Eckart,
Bernd Hilpert,
Kathrin Krell,
Jochen Leinberger

Grafik und Illustration
Bernd Hilpert,
Kathrin Krell,
Christiane Both

Produktion
Bruno Scheffler,
Christiane Both

Architektur
Arge Wetterpark (unit-design und bb22 Architekten und Stadtplaner)

Verantwortlich
Bernd Hilpert,
Peter Eckart

Architektonische Beratung Entwurf
Boris Banozic

Architektonische Beratung Planung
Jan Schulz

Grafikproduktion
Macholz und Heidergott, Schäffer und Peters (Turm)

Meteorologische Fachberatung
Deutscher Wetterdienst
Gerhard Lux,
Ulrike Rupprecht,
Armin Pfennig

Stahlbau Turm
Laudemann GmbH, Sontra

Bau, Generalunternehmer
Ambrosius Messebau
Christian Buesgen

Landschaftsbau
Immo Herbst

Seite 42-43

Titel
„Walk of Ideas" – ein Spaziergang durch Ideen aus Deutschland

Thema / Produkt
Kommunikation von Deutschland als „Land der Ideen"

Auftraggeber
FC Deutschland GmbH, Berlin
Mike de Vries

Werbeleitung
Dr. Ronald Seeliger

Designagentur
Scholz & Friends Sensai

Creative Direction
Wolf Schneider

Executive Direction
Tobias Wolff

Art Direction
Jürgen Krugsperger,
Andreas Bergmann,
Alf Speidel,
Danielle Sellin,
Christian Rühe,
Nicolaus von Hantelmann,
Ralph Bremenkamp,
Claus Potthoff
(Audi AG),
Stephan Dietrich
(adidas Salomon AG)

Strategische Planung
Penelope Winterhager

Text
Katherine Ossenkopp,
Mirko Derpmann

Kundenberater
Wolf Schneider

Filmproduktion
United Visions TV & Film Productions,
John Bandmann

Regie
Jörg Wienforth

Kamera
Kai Rostasy

Producer
Ulrike Peckskamp

Schnitt
Andrea Guggenberger

Sound
Audioforce

Produktdesign
Wolf Schneider

Architektur
Wolf Schneider,
Tobias Wolff

Fotografie Architektur
Eberle & Eisfeld

Creative Direction
Matthias Spaetgens

Art Director
Frederik Hofmann

Fotografie Bildband
Stephan Erfurt

Creative Direction
Petra Reichenbach

INDEX

AWARD

Seite 46-47

Titel
Oerlikon – We are one

Auftraggeber
**OC Oerlikon
Management AG
Thomas P. Limberger,
Andreas Harting,
Stefan Sell**

Designagentur
Claus Koch™

Creative Direction
**Claus Koch
Michael Mehler
Frank Mueller**

Art Direction
**Susanne Büker
Patrick Koch**

Text Anzeigen
Patrick Koch

Typografie
**Patrick Koch
Michael Mehler
Frank Mueller**

Kundenberatung
**Waltraud Teleu
Susanna von Simson
Sonja Ney**

Videoproduktion
**Markenfilm Zürich
Heinrich Reinacher,
Uli Scheper**

Creative Direction
Patrick Koch

Cutting
Freischwimmer

Messedesign / Airport
**Claus Koch
Patrick Koch
Frank Mueller**

Fotografie
**Tim Thiel
Archiv Oerlikon**

Seite 48-49

Titel
**Die Audi
Messekommunikation:
„Audi A-Messe-Konzept"**

Thema / Produkt
Automobil

Auftraggeber
**Audi AG,
Bernhard Neumann**

Designagentur
Mutabor Design GmbH

Creative Direction
**Johannes Plass
Heinrich Paravicini**

Projektleitung
**Christian Dworak
Axel Domke
Jessica Hoppe
Frederike Putz**

Design
**Simone Breckner
Simone Campe
Patrick Meny
Patrick Molinari
Kai Riemland
Malte Schweers
Nils Zimmermann**

Produktdesign
**Mutabor Design GmbH,
Peter Kettenring**

Architektur
Schmidhuber + Partner

Fotografie
Diverse

GOLD

Seite 78-79

Titel
**U-Bahnhof Lohring,
Bochum**

Auftraggeber
**Bochum-Gelsenkirche-
ner Stadtbahnverpach-
tungsgesellschaft des
bürgerlichen Rechts**

Verantwortlich
**Tiefbauamt der
Stadt Bochum,
Abteilung Stadtbahn
Karl-Heinz Reikat**

Kunst & Musik,
Kunstkonzept
Eva-Maria Joeressen

Kunst & Musik,
Klanginstallation
Klaus Kessner

Architektur
**RÜBSAMEN + PARTNER
ARCHITEKTEN BDA
INGENIEURE
Holger Rübsamen
Boris E. Biskamp**

Mitarbeit (Wettbewerb)
Sascha Hinz

Fotografie
Lukas Roth

Mobiliar
**RÜBSAMEN + PARTNER
ARCHITEKTEN BDA
INGENIEURE
Holger Rübsamen
Boris E. Biskamp**

Entwickelt und ausgeführt
Hess Form + Licht

Seite 80-81

Titel
**Der Meissen ab 18
Kalender**

Thema / Produkt
Meissener Porzellan

Auftraggeber
**Staatliche
Porzellan-Manufaktur
Meissen GmbH
Wolfgang Kolitsch**

Designagentur
Scholz & Friends, Berlin

Creative Direction
**Martin Pross
Raphael Püttmann
Mario Gamper**

Art Direction
Anje Jager

Text
Stephan Deisenhofer

Kundenberater
**Jörg Mayer
Michael Schulze**

Grafik
Melanie Fischbach

Producer
**Anikó Krüger,
Scholz & Friends**

Bildbearbeitung
**Andreas Freitag,
BerlinPostproduction**

Fotografie
**Attila Hartwig c/o
Nerger Mao**

Seite 82-83

Titel
„Nonplusultra"

Thema / Produkt
Wandkalender 2006

Auftraggeber
Papierfabrik Scheufelen
GmbH + Co. KG
Irmgard Glanz

Designagentur
Strichpunkt

Creative Direction
Kirsten Dietz
Jochen Rädeker

Art Direction
Kirsten Dietz

Designer
Susanne Hörner
Felix Widmaier

Kundenberater
Jochen Rädeker

Druckerei
Grafisches Zentrum
Drucktechnik,
Ditzingen-Heimerdingen

Illustration
Susanne Hörner

Seite 84-85

Titel
ALcom Series

Thema / Produkt
Tisch- und Bank-
programm

Auftraggeber
ONE by ONE Co., Ltd.

Designagentur
f/p design gmbh

Produktdesign
Fritz Frenkler
Anette Ponholzer

Seite 86-87

Titel
SZ Krimi Bibliothek

Auftraggeber
Süddeutsche Zeitung
GmbH
Klaus Füreder
Sonja Assfalg
Thi-Nga Tang

Creative Direction
Alexander Bartel
Martin Kießling

Art Direction
Zeljko Pezely

Text
Marcel Koop

Kundenberater
Clemens Dreyer
Florine Falkenstein

Fotografie
Jan Willem Scholten

Seite 88-89

Titel
Audi R8

Thema / Produkt
Audi R8

Auftraggeber
Audi AG,
Dr. Marc A. Caesar

Designagentur
argonauten G2 GmbH

Creative Direction
Sven Küster

Art Direction
Oliver Hinrichs

Technical Manager
Oliver List

Technical Supervisor
Sven Gessner

Kundenberater
Christina Fiedler
Mathias Sinn

Senior Technical Consultant
Dorian Roy

Seite 90-91

Titel
10 Jahre A&W-
Designer des Jahres
Cover

Auftraggeber
A&W
Architektur&Wohnen
Barbara Friedrich
Chefredakteurin

Art Direction
Thomas Elmenhorst

Fotografie
Uli Weber,
Alastair Thain,
Kay Degenhard,
Maria Vittoria
Backhaus,
Francesco Astori,
Tom Nagy,
John Davis,
Giovanni Castell,
Christian Grund

Verlag
JAHRESZEITEN
VERLAG GMBH

SILBER

Seite 94-95

Titel
Scharfe Messer

Thema / Produkt
WMF GrandGourmet-
Messer

Auftraggeber
WMF AG
Wolfgang Dalferth

Designagentur
KNSK

Creative Direction
Niels Holle
Tim Krink

Art Direction
Jörg-Thomas Thiele

Text
Steffen Steffens
Berend Brüdgam

Typografie
Jörg-Thomas Thiele

Kundenberater
Kirsten Kohls

DTP-Studio
ABC Digital
Holger Ittershagen

Verlag
WMF Hauspresse

Fotografie
Markus Heumann